I Pinky Promise

Kelly Samples McNew

This book is dedicated to…
My dad, who has always been my superhero.
My mom, who has always been my best friend.
My brother, who has always been my role model.

The Pinky Promise

Standing in front of him, looking into the eyes of the man who had changed my life forever. I reached out my hand, stuck out my pinky, and anticipated what he was going to do next. This man's decision, in this moment, would determine whether or not I found hope or disappointment.

A pinky promise is a commitment made with the deepest sincerity. It's not just any old, ordinary promise. It's a binding agreement that indicates a mutual expectation. If a Pinky Promise is broken, there are serious repercussions and a hefty loss of trust.

It's as if the world taints you from thinking that it's possible for someone to keep their word just by making a Pinky Promise.

I truly believe that this world is full of goodness and people who can be trusted to do what they say they will do -- especially when bound by a Pinky Promise. It is the ultimate, most powerful promise of all.

The Little Girl

Born and raised in Bagdad, Kentucky, I had a country twang from the time I started talking.

My life was the typical American dream. I always had my mom and dad to take care of me and my older brother to pick on me. Matthew, my brother, is eight years older than I, so he could pin me down and tickle me until I couldn't breathe.

When I was born, we lived on a farm with cows. I was taking the calves milk by the time I was four years old. I grew up as a tomboy. Like any typical Kentuckian, I wore my baseball cap backwards and never liked to wear shoes. I spent every day outside, getting dirty in the mud. But I never, ever would get my hands dirty.

Even though I was a tomboy, my favorite color was purple. This was the color my daddy always told me looked the best on me. I had my dad wrapped around my little finger, and we were best buds. He taught me how to ride a bike and how to play softball. He would be at every single basketball game, cheering me on. He was the one who woke me up every morning for school and did my hair, until he accidentally burned my ear with the curling iron… I never let him get near me with a curling iron again.

My dad was the Director of Disaster Emergency Services for Shelby County, and he worked many long days. He was never home during severe weather, tornado warnings, anthrax threats, or any emergency that pertained to the safety of the people. He spent most of his time taking care of everyone else instead of himself.

Before I was born, he was an Emergency Medical Technician (EMT). He has always worked to save lives. Some of my favorite memories were going to work with him on Saturdays or during the summer. When we would go to lunch, he let me ride with him in the ambulance and he would always let me pick where to eat.

By the time I was eight years old, I wanted to be just like my daddy when I grew up. I wanted to help other people, but I didn't really want to be an EMT or work in hospitals because I don't like the sight of blood.

I wasn't quite sure what I wanted to be when I grew up, but some things I knew for sure: I was a daddy's girl, a country girl, and a tough girl. Most of all, I was a little girl who wanted to grow up and do something big to help others – just like my dad.

Something BIG

My parents always told me, "You can be anything you want to be when you grow up." It sounds super cliché, and as we get older, we may start to think it's not completely true. But, yet maybe it is.

As a six-year-old die-hard Reba McEntire fan, I thought I wanted to be a famous country music singer. Even though, I can't even sing on key. Then, I thought I wanted to become a horse jockey. But I had only ridden on a horse one time.

By the seventh grade, I started thinking about work in public service. I dreamed of being the first woman to work with the Disaster Emergency Services in Shelby County, and that way I'd follow in my daddy's footsteps. Then I thought about becoming a sheriff's deputy, but a lot of people would argue that I was not intimidating or strong enough to be a good deputy. Despite my various interests, one thing was for sure… my desire to help others was stronger than ever.

There are so many opportunities in this big world, and I don't want to miss out on any of them.

When I was really young, I was terrified thinking about how the world was so big. It was hard to imagine people in China sleeping while people in my neighborhood were going about their daily activities; or someone climbing Mt. Everest while I watched TV. It's difficult to imagine that the world is so big with so many people doing so many different things at the same time.

When I looked at the globe in my third grade classroom, I thought of myself as just a small insignificant piece in this big, big world. But, in my daddy's eyes, I was the biggest, most important thing in this huge world. I knew that there were more people in this world than I could even count or imagine. It only stands to reason, since this world is so big, there has to be something bigger than I, bigger than us.

I grew up going to church every Sunday and every Wednesday night. I learned Bible stories in Sunday School class. We recited Bible verses and studied the real meaning of Christmas and Easter. I learned that there was not *something* bigger, but *someONE* bigger. There is *someONE* greater than me and greater than this world. There *is someONE* who is greater than we can ever imagine, and that *someONE* is God.

Some people don't believe that there is anything or anyone beyond us. There are those who think that when we die on this earth, that's the end. There is nothing more. Then, there are others who believe that the world works like a perpetual spinning wheel, with each life coming back as a different human being, flower, or animal. Some people don't believe in the power of prayer. They think that the stories in the Bible are merely stories. Those same people don't believe in miracles either.

These people haven't seen what I've seen or felt what I've felt. They don't know the story of my life.

My story is one that is not well-known, but it is a story in which God is definitely apparent. It goes a little something like this...

We were "good" people living our everyday lives with work, school, church, family dinners, and bedtime prayers. My brother and I planned to be the best people we could while helping as many people as we could, which are the values that my parents had always instilled in us. However, this did not make us immune to the evils in this world. My family did not avoid the punishment of sin simply because of our good works. If anything, our tragedies have hit us like a thief in the night. Troubles came when we least expected them and still took nearly everything we had.

Metaphorically speaking, I wish our house had an alarm system to warn us when something bad was about to happen. I wasn't ready for it when it came. None of us were. However, we were blessed because *someONE* bigger was there to take care of us.

Lazarus

Over the last fifty years, numerous people have told their stories of being dead and coming back to life. Once they come back, they tell stories of what they experienced in the afterlife. People brought back from death might tell you they saw a bright light or heard a loud sound. They may have seen loved ones who have already passed or guardian angels who watch over them. Some may have out-of-body experiences where they are able to step back and see themselves. Such stories are not uncommon. Of course, there are scientists who argue that the images people see or the experiences they have are simply the brain chemically responding to stress.

I will admit that it is difficult to hear someone tell their story of a near-death experience and not wonder how much of it is true. We don't want to question it, but there is a little voice of hesitation speaking inside of us. How can we believe what is unseen or not proven? Sometimes it is hard for us to believe that God still performs miracles. We read about miracles that Jesus performed in the Bible over 2000 years ago. However, we are often guilty of not giving credit to God for the miracles He performs in our lives every single day.

In the Gospel of John, the fourth book of the New Testament, there is an account of a man named Lazarus who was raised from the dead. This was one of the stories I learned in Sunday School as a little girl. Lazarus was very sick. His sisters, Mary and Martha, called for Jesus to come to them and heal their brother. However, when Jesus arrived, it was too late. Lazarus was already in the tomb, wrapped in linens, dead for four days. At first, Martha and Mary spoke with Jesus and told Him how they wished He had been there sooner to save their brother. Jesus did not let their wishes or grief distract Him. He told them to roll the stone away from Lazarus' tomb. Martha was very quick to state how they should not roll the stone away because of the bad odor that would be present with a dead and decaying body. Martha did not doubt Jesus' power, but she didn't think it was possible for her brother to be alive inside the tomb. Then Jesus called for Lazarus to come out. The dead man walked out of the tomb and was alive again. This is one of God's miracles.

I am blessed to be able to tell you the story about my dad which closely resembles Lazarus' story. My dad was dead, without a heartbeat, without a pulse, and without a breath for nearly an hour. Like Lazarus, he was called back to life. My dad is one of God's miracles.

His Heart Stopped Beating

It was August 2, 2002. I was ten years old and getting ready to start the sixth grade. When my mom and I pulled into the driveway, something didn't feel right. My dad's white Explorer was there. He never came home early from work.

The night before, my mom and dad had been arguing. Walking into the house was like walking into church late on Sunday morning; you tiptoe and try not to make a noise. My dad was lying on the couch with an afghan and a two-liter of Diet

Mountain Dew -- his favorite soft drink. My mom asked him what he was doing home, and all he said was that he didn't feel well.

My mom and I left my dad alone and he went back to the bedroom to take a nap. My mom went to clean up the kitchen while I started painting something for my grandma. After a few minutes, my mom came in to check on my progress when we heard a loud, obnoxious snoring sound. We both looked at each other wondering what we were hearing.

My mother hastily stammered, "He couldn't be asleep that fast." She barely finished her sentence when she realized what was happening and bolted toward the bedroom. I followed right behind her but didn't have a clue about what was going on.

When she ran through the bedroom door, she threw herself on top of my father who was lying on the floor, jerking, gasping for air. She started screaming his name, "Jack! Jack!" We both went toward the phone to call 9-1-1. Mom ran to the phone in the bedroom, and I ran to the phone in the kitchen. It was one of those moments when you don't have a clue what you're doing. I just stared at the phone for a few seconds and didn't know which buttons to press.

My mom dialed 9-1-1 first and yelled for me to come and help her. She told me to look for Nitroglycerin, a heart medicine that my dad always carried in his pocket. I pulled out coins and napkins from his pants pockets but couldn't find the pills. As my mom realized it was too late for the medicine to help, she told me to try to turn him over on his back so she could start CPR. She was telling the dispatcher where we lived, and I'll never forget her saying, "It's Jack Samples. Tell them to hurry!" The ones responding to the 9-1-1 call, the ones coming to try and save my daddy, were the best friends he had worked with his entire life.

I grabbed my dad's shoulders and tried to put him on his back, but I couldn't move him. I felt like I was making things worse because his body kept jerking forward. I called to him over and over. "Daddy. Daddy!" Honestly, I really hoped he was faking it. It didn't seem real. It was like nothing I had experienced before. I had never heard such noises nor had I ever seen anyone's body convulse like his body was convulsing. I kept shouting and crying and wishing that it wasn't real.

My mom finally got off the phone with 9-1-1. She wanted to get me out of the room. She told me to go get help from our neighbor, Mark Coleman. At the time, I thought I was helping by getting someone, but really she just didn't want me there to see my daddy so sick.

I ran out the front door and sprinted as fast as I could to the neighbor's house. My dog, 9ball, ran alongside me and knocked me down just before I crossed the road. I jumped back up and kept running. When I got to the neighbor's house, I didn't even knock on the front door. I burst through it, screaming for anyone who could help us. Mark was there. I yelled, "Come quick! Something is wrong with my dad! He's sick! Mom said we need your help." He told me to go ahead and he would be right behind me.

I took off again across the road and back to my house. I had no idea what I would find when I returned. The first responders were already coming into our home. More trucks with lights were pulling into our driveway. My mom stayed with daddy the whole time. I'm sure she had yelled, beat on his chest, and tried to start CPR. When I got to the house, the first responders wouldn't let me see him. I was the little girl pacing on our living room floor while people walked past me with defibrillators and big bags. After what seemed like forever, the paramedics arrived. They pulled the stretcher through our front door with tears rolling down their faces. They knew where they were and who their patient was.

I was holding Molly, my favorite doll, when my dad's cell phone started ringing. At first, I just looked at it. It started ringing again. I picked it up and saw that it was one of my dad's coworkers. He knew something was wrong and asked if my dad was okay. I was getting mad because he sounded so calm on the phone, acting like everything was okay.

He had heard our address go across the scanner and wondered if the emergency was at our house. I screamed into the phone, "No, he's not okay! He can't talk right now!" Then I hung up, throwing the phone across the room.

Mark walked through the front door and came right over to me. His job was to get me and my mom out of the house and out of the way, and to take us to the hospital. My mom didn't want to leave. She was fighting back. I didn't want to go either. I kept yelling as loud as I could, "I love you daddy." Hoping he could hear me, I wanted to tell him that I loved him one more time.

After five minutes of fighting back, Mark was finally able to get both of us into the car. We headed toward the Shelbyville hospital. My mom kept looking behind us as we were driving away. I remembered her hands shaking. She couldn't sit still and was gasping for air. As she looked behind us, she kept saying, "They're not coming. I don't see any lights. He's not going to make it. He's dead."

She kept saying it over and over. I was crying uncontrollably.

At that moment, I thought it was over. I thought I was never going to see my dad again. We were six miles down the road, and my mom asked Mark to pull over to the side. She couldn't breathe. She was having a panic attack. Mark kept telling my mom that we had to get her to the hospital. She was doubled over on the side of the road, gasping for air. Within a few minutes, we looked back to see the ambulance pop up over the top of the hill. It was coming fast with its lights on. It zoomed past us. My mom jumped back into the car. There was a glimmer of hope that maybe my dad would be okay. We couldn't see inside the ambulance, so we didn't know what was going on. We could see lots of people standing up in the back, but we couldn't see my dad.

What I didn't know, was that his heart had stopped beating. He had no pulse.

My Prayer

When we got to the hospital, I was rushed into a secretary's office where I had to sit by myself. The paramedics were bringing my dad out of the ambulance. My mom had to be given medicine because she was so worked up and had made herself sick. I sat alone in that small secretary's office for what seemed like forever, but really was only a few minutes.

My brother had been at work, but I think someone called to tell him to get to the hospital. Someone must have called all of our family members, because when I peeked out into the hallway, there was my Granny B, Granddaddy, aunts, uncles, and lots of other people. Then I saw my brother. He came toward me, picked me up off the ground, and wrapped his arms around me. He understood everything that was happening, and he also knew that I didn't understand anything. He held on to me tightly and assured me that everything was going to be okay.

As he sat me down, he rushed me back to the office with his boss, Beth Simmons, her daughter, and my cousin Kate. We stood in the office just staring at each other. I finally broke the silence and said that we should say a prayer. The four of us gathered together, held hands, and bowed our heads. I remember every word of that prayer, and I remember that was the closest I had ever felt talking to God.

"Dear God, please let my daddy be okay.
Please let him be there to see me graduate from
middle school.
Please let him be there to see me graduate from
high school and college.

Please let him be there to walk me down the aisle."

Beth Simmons stopped my prayer and giggled, telling me not to be silly. As a ten year old girl, it may have been a little ridiculous for me to be praying about my college graduation and wedding day, but I wanted my daddy to be there for all of those important things. I didn't want him to miss any of them.

We talked for a few more minutes while trying to avoid the obvious conversation. Then someone flung open the office door and yelled, "They have a heartbeat!!!!" My dad was not stable, but they were going to transport him to a hospital in Louisville where they would do surgery.

I ran out of the office and clung to my brother. They asked us if we wanted to see him before he left. We didn't even hesitate.

As we walked back through the emergency room doors, we were met by our mom; she didn't look so good, either. The emergency room staff tried to prepare us for what we would see next, telling us that he wouldn't look like our dad right now. Nothing they said prepared me for what I saw as I walked into that room where my dad was laying on the stretcher.

I had to make myself look, and then I had to continue telling myself that my dad was the one lying there. Cords were attached all over him. Machines were beeping. Lines and numbers were flashing over the monitor. He looked lifeless. Someone was pumping oxygen into his mouth every few seconds. I stood right there next to my dad and was in complete and utter shock because none of this made any sense to me.

If my dad had a heartbeat, then I thought he would be able to open his eyes and look at me. I thought he would at least be able to tell me that he loves me. He couldn't do any of those things. I was afraid to step too close to him because I didn't want to hit any of the cords. There were so many other people in the room. We weren't allowed to stay in the room for very long because the medical staff was trying to load him into the ambulance.

I quickly reached out to touch his hand before they wheeled him away; I barely got to run my fingers across it. His hand didn't feel like my daddy's hand. It was clammy, stiff, and didn't conform to mine. This didn't seem like the hand that picked me up when I fell down, or the one that held my bike up straight while I learned to ride without training wheels. It didn't feel like the hand that held on to me tight for hugs while tucking me in at night. It was hard to believe that this was my dad.

Tiger Tucker, the chief of the Shelbyville Fire Department, drove me, my mom, and my brother to the hospital in Louisville. I sat in the back seat with my brother. The car was so quiet. I just sat there, completely scared to death. The question hanging in the air that no one wanted to ask, is Dad going to be okay? We were afraid of the answer. I wasn't really sure what was going on and what was going to happen when we arrived at the hospital.

Someone must have called the police department to block the roads so we could get to the hospital quicker, because at each intersection there was a police car blocking traffic. Once we were on the interstate, we followed right behind the ambulance. I looked down at the speedometer and it read over 100 miles per hour. I had never been in a car that was moving that fast.

Most of all, I was scared that my daddy would never come home again. Even though he had a heartbeat, I was afraid I would lose the man that I had always known as my superhero.

Waiting

As we entered the waiting room, I had no idea how long we were going to be there. We were all just supposed to sit there and wait. For my mom that meant pacing, sitting down, and standing right back up again. At first they had all of us in the waiting room, but later they directed us to a separate room where we could wait together with just our family and friends. We anxiously awaited for news, any news.

Dad was in surgery. We waited there for hours. At this point, I overheard someone explain that he had had a massive heart attack and mentioned the previous stints that were put in when I was so little I couldn't remember it. People in the waiting room weren't really saying anything to me.

I just sat there listening to everyone else talk like I wasn't in the room.

It started getting dark outside, and some of our friends offered to take me and my brother downstairs to get something to eat. They had heard my stomach starting to grumble. My mom stayed behind. She just wanted to stay in our waiting area, in case my dad needed her.

A group of seven of us walked downstairs to eat overpriced sandwiches, which I didn't even feel like eating. An hour later, we made it back upstairs and my mom said that the doctor had come out to talk with her while we were gone. She wasn't smiling. She started crying again as she began to share the news.

Doctors don't seem to sugarcoat anything or worry about a family's feelings to bring any form of peace when giving an update. Their blunt explanation to my mother was that my dad was out of surgery, and they were able to put stints in the blockages; however, he was now in a coma. The doctor explained that he didn't know if Dad would come out of the coma in a few hours, days, or if ever.

My dad would most likely be a vegetable on a ventilator for the rest of his life. He was without oxygen for such a long period of time that part of his brain had died. The doctors were unsure if he would be able to make any kind of recovery.

While we were eating, my mom got to walk back to see him. She talked to him, but he didn't respond. She squeezed his hand, but he didn't move. He lay there with the machine breathing for him, hooked up to IV's, and all of the monitors beeping.

Our family was left alone to wait... and wait.

Someone Else's Home

My mom didn't come home with my brother and me that night. She slept in a chair in the waiting room. I doubt she really slept at all. My aunt and uncle drove us home. On the way home was when everything really started sinking in. It came over me all at once and tears just started pouring from my eyes and wouldn't stop.

I didn't want to go home. When we pulled into our driveway, I didn't want to go inside. My dad's white Ford Explorer sat in the driveway, and it was just another reminder that he wouldn't be there to tuck me in that night.

Our dog, 9ball, barked at us as soon as we got out of the car. He had never barked at us before, so he must have known something was wrong. As I walked through the backdoor, it was like walking into someone else's home. It didn't feel like the same place where I had grown up. I was the first one to start walking through all of the rooms. My brother followed me. There was stuff scattered everywhere. When we got to my parent's bedroom, I showed Matthew where Dad had been lying. There were clothes, coins, tissues, and stuff from my dad's pockets thrown all over the floor. We didn't touch anything. We just left it alone as if that's where things were supposed to be. I was scared to step on the spot where Dad had fallen. I kept jumping over it. It was as if I was treating it like a grave at a cemetery.

My brother and I tried to go to sleep, but counting sheep didn't make sleep come any easier; it was nearly impossible. It was as if I was trying to sleep in someone else's home. It didn't feel like my family's home. Everything was different.

A Vegetable

Dad was in a coma.

He was on a lot of medication, so I thought he was just sleeping it off. The reality was that no one knew when, or if, he would ever wake up. I got to see him the next day when Matthew and I went back to the hospital. His skin was an icky gray color, he wasn't moving, and the machines just kept beeping. I tried to look at all the machines and buttons around the room because it hurt too much to look at him lying stiff in the bed. He was in the Intensive Care Unit, indefinitely.

A few days later they inserted a feeding tube. My mom was staying there every night and sleeping in hospital chairs. Every night Matthew and I would go home, and Mom and I would say night-time prayers over the phone. Every night we would pray that Dad would wake up from his coma and everything would be okay.

After a few weeks, he still was not awake. They decided to perform a tracheotomy. They made an incision in his throat and put a tube in so there would be direct access to his windpipe. It seemed as if he was just living off of a machine.

A few more weeks passed. I started the sixth grade. My mom still hadn't come home from the hospital. She took showers in hospital rooms and barely ate enough to stay alive. My brother started college. My aunts took turns staying with me at my house.

One time, my mom left the hospital for the night and stayed with me in a hotel. Of course, it was the one closest to the hospital. There is only one thing I remember about that night. We got to the hotel room late because we had stayed at the hospital as long as the nurses would let us. Before we went to sleep, my mom and I sat on the bed; she looked at me and said, "Kelly, your dad may always be like this." I knew she was about to cry, so I stopped her from saying anything else.

I didn't cry that night in the hotel room. My mom needed me to be strong just like she had always been strong for me.

I had always heard everything the doctors said while they talked to my mom. They gave my dad no hope. According to the doctors, he was going to be a vegetable for the rest of his life. When he had his heart attack, he had gone too long without oxygen and there was too much brain damage. I spent days and days at the hospital, sitting with my dad. I talked to him, told him stories, and even asked him about my math homework. Even though he never talked back, never smiled, never made any noise, and never moved, I still didn't believe what the doctors were saying. Maybe it was because I was ten years old and it didn't feel real, or maybe I was being too optimistic. I just knew that I didn't want my dad to be like this.

That night at the hotel my mom and I said our nightly prayers, like every other night, and prayed that Dad would be okay.

Kindred

Once you are on a ventilator, with a trach, and in a coma for a long time, the doctors generally move you to a long-term care facility. My dad was sent to Kindred Hospital in Louisville, Kentucky. This was the only option my mom was given because the doctors could no longer do anything for my dad. Everything about Kindred looked and felt bad.

The outside of the building looked like a scary, abandoned house that you might see in the movies. On the outside there weren't many people around. On the inside, it felt like a haunted house where someone might jump out at you at any minute. No one in the building looked happy.

My dad didn't deal very well with the move. Neither did my mom. She wasn't allowed to stay at this facility overnight. She had to come home but she wasn't ready to leave him.

When she first walked through the door to our house, she went straight to the place where my dad had fallen and dropped to her knees. She sat there and sobbed for nearly an hour. She called the hospital every night before we went to bed, but it took the nurses forever to answer. The phone would ring and ring and no one would pick up. Every single time they would answer, she would ask for the nurses to go in and check on him.

The good thing about my mom being at home was that she dropped me off at school every morning. Then she spent the rest of her day at Kindred with my dad. After school I would hang out with aunts, cousins, or friends of the family. My mom would pick me up once visiting hours were over. I got to go see my dad a couple times a week but not as often as I wanted to.

I would rather have been sitting at Kindred with my dad than pretending to care about school. Every time the phone rang in our class, I would get this anxious bombshell feeling in my stomach, hoping the call would be for me. I would daydream about my mom calling the school and them calling me down to the office to tell me my dad was awake. Each day I wished that the phone would ring, and each day I prayed that my dad would be better. He didn't need to be in Kindred anymore. All my mom would say is how much she hated that place.

Eleven Candles

September 19th… I turned eleven. Before my dad's heart attack, I had asked him for a horse, and I really think that was going to be my birthday present. By the time my birthday actually came around, I didn't care anything about the day or the horse. It was just another day that my dad wasn't home.

My dad had been in a coma for 48 days-- almost seven weeks. I couldn't believe how much he missed out on in this short time. He didn't know that I had made the sixth grade basketball team. He had no idea how well I was doing in my classes. He didn't get to move my brother into college.

We celebrated my eleventh birthday in the hospital with my dad. My mom got me a few presents to open, which I'm pretty sure that my aunt picked out. The only one I can remember is a cd holder. We had a small cake, and my mom sang "Happy Birthday" to me. We pretended to have a lit candle. At the very end of the song I made my wish. I wished that my dad would wake up from his coma and everything would go back to normal.

Amen

I've always thought of wishes as prayers without an amen. If you think about it, wishes really are just us asking for things we want, which is often what we find ourselves doing when we pray. God knows our wishes, the same as He knows our prayers.

When bad things happen, prayer brings us closer to God and closer to everyone around us. People join together in prayer as a way to support a friend or family as they seek comfort and peace during difficult times. With believers, prayer is our most intimate communication with God. It is also the most special gift that can be offered to someone in a time of need.

My family and I clung to prayer. Talking to God was the only thing that kept us sane. We looked to Him for strength and direction. He provided for us enough courage and strength to get out of bed every morning and He helped carry us through each day.

The amount of support, prayer, and help my family received after my dad's heart attack was remarkable. It was absolutely humbling to have so many cards, visits, phone calls, and open arms stretched out, ready to embrace my family. At the time, I didn't realize how many people had rearranged their lives and were so willing to help take care of me. Hard times like these make you realize how blessed you really are, and I just want to take this moment to say thank you. You all know who you are.

Our small town of Bagdad decided to hold a prayer service in honor of my dad at the church he had gone to since he was a little boy, Bagdad Baptist. It was on September 21, two days after my birthday. That Saturday night people flooded through the church doors and the pews were packed. I sat on one of the front pews with almost everyone in our family. For over an hour, we were in the sanctuary spending time in prayer, meditation, singing hymns, and talking with God. We prayed that God would be with my family. We prayed that God would be with my dad. We prayed that my dad would wake up from his coma and get better. We prayed that my dad would make a full recovery. We prayed and we prayed, Lord be with us. Amen.

Two Days Later

Two days after the prayer service, four days after
my birthday, my dad had another surgery. He was
still at Kindred Hospital, and they were downsizing
the trach in his throat. So many wishes and so many
prayers had been said in these past few days.

Phyllis Bailey, a nice lady from Bagdad,
came to pick me up from school. She took me to
McDonalds to get a Happy Meal. We were in line,
ready to order, and the phone rang. My mom was
calling, which she usually did as soon as I got out of

school. Instead of her usual questions about how my school day went she said, "Your dad's awake!"

I think I jumped so high that my shoes nearly came off my feet! My first question was if I could come and see him.

My mom told me that I should wait until tomorrow when she would be able to bring me down to the hospital. She told me that she would call me later, but she had to go see how Dad was doing. I ran back inside McDonalds and couldn't stop jumping up and down. All I kept saying was, "Dad's awake! Dad's awake!" I was screaming the news to people that I didn't even know. I even got up on one of the chairs.

It didn't seem real. That was the moment in my life when I sincerely needed someone to pinch me to make sure I wasn't dreaming. My dad was awake from his coma! He had proven the doctors wrong. God answered our prayers and granted our wishes!

At this moment I truly thought that my dad would be exactly the same as he had always been. I thought I would go down to the hospital the next day, sit on his knee, and tell him everything that he had missed out on. I was expecting a huge hug from him and never letting go. In the movies, when people woke up from a coma they were the same, so I thought my dad would be the same. This wasn't the movies, and my dad wasn't the same.

The Day My Dad Started Over

I was getting a weird feeling from my mom. It seemed like she didn't want me to go to the hospital to see my dad. She said he was different than before, but I didn't really understand what she meant by "different." It was like she was trying to warn me, but she just couldn't come out and say it.

After walking into his hospital room that next day, I don't know if my dad really knew that I was there. He was awake and he was kind of talking. The words coming out of his mouth didn't make a lot of sense. His voice sounded different; he didn't sound like I remembered or what I had heard in the old home movies that I had been watching. He didn't seem happy and it was like he was very confused. I think I was confused too because I didn't understand what was wrong.

When I first saw him, the nurse was trying to sit him up on the side of the bed. He was pulling against the nurse though, so she laid him back down. I tried to say hi to him but I was really nervous, so I just sat and watched for a while. His eyes were wandering everywhere and it seemed as if he didn't have control of his body. His head would roll around like a newborn that couldn't control their neck muscles. It was like he was trying to get up, but his body just wouldn't let him.

For some reason, my dad thought he was 28 years old again, which was how old he was when he and my mom got married. He also thought his nurse was his wife, so he didn't understand who my mom was and why she was there. I thought, since he had forgotten about the past twelve years of his life that he may have forgotten about me. He assured me that he knew I was his daughter, Kelly.

The doctors and nurses tried to keep my dad still. At first they strapped down his arms and legs, but that didn't work for very long. I didn't like it when they did that because it looked like they were treating my dad as a prisoner. They put him in a new hospital bed that looked like a cage. There was netting all around the sides and on top of it. They said it was for his protection to keep him from falling out, but I really think it was because the nurses didn't want to have to keep an eye on him all the time. My mom hated the new bed because almost every morning when she got to the hospital, my dad was half way down the bed. His head would be in the middle and his legs would be curled up to one side, with his body crumpled up. He just couldn't lie still.

At this point, I knew that my dad was different than before, and he would never be the

same man I knew prior to his heart attack. I was
kind of sad, but at the same time I knew I shouldn't
be sad; my dad was alive. Even as he was lying in
the hospital bed, I was proud to say that I am his
daughter. It didn't matter that my dad was different
now. I was going to love my dad no matter what.

My mom tried to explain to me what would
happen next. They were already talking about
transferring him to a hospital with a rehab facility
where he would have to relearn everything. He
didn't know how to walk or roll over or pick
himself up. He wasn't able to say what he wanted to
say because his mouth wouldn't let him form the
words. He had lost so much muscle mass and
basically had no strength at all.

One of the toughest things he would have to
learn was how to do all of these things that he didn't
know how to do--in the dark. My dad had lost his
eyesight. When he first woke up from the coma, we
thought he could tell the difference between light
and dark, but after a few days, we weren't so sure.
Once the doctors did some tests, they were able to

tell us that my dad's eyes were perfectly fine. The problem was that his brain couldn't tell him what he was seeing; that part of his brain had died when he was without oxygen. Whatever the reason, my dad was blind.

No one in my family knew what the next days and months would be like. I don't know if anyone in my family was really ready to handle everything that was ahead of us. My dad was forty-four years old, and he was going to have to start from the beginning, learning everything all over. I think we knew it wasn't going to be easy, and, of course, it was going to be frustrating for him. This was a man who loved to help everyone and give and do as much as he could, but now he was going to have to rely on everyone else to help him. He wasn't used to having people do everything for him. The day my dad woke up from his coma was the day that my dad started over.

Baby
Steps

Within the week my dad was sent to Frazier
Rehabilitation Hospital, which is known for its
extensive and intensive rehab programs. He spent
the majority of his day in some type of therapy. He
had physical therapy, occupational therapy, speech
therapy. There was a long list of things he had to
work on. My mom went with him everywhere. She
wanted to be there so she would know how to help
him with these things when he came home.

After a while, he finally realized my mom
was his wife and stopped talking to the nurse like
she was his honey; his memory was slowly coming
back. The therapists helped him work on recovering

his memory during therapy, too. They asked him his name, his birthday, questions about our family, and other details from his life to get his mind working.

In the first weeks at the Frazier Rehab Facility, he was completely bound to a wheelchair. He couldn't sit up yet on his own. The first time he stood up while holding onto a walker was a pretty big deal. He couldn't stand up very long, but every single day the therapists would push him to work a little bit longer. Sometimes he would get sad and not want to do any of his therapy, especially when he would fall or couldn't do certain things the therapists asked. He would get so upset and worked up about things that he would start to shake uncontrollably. It scared me sometimes when he acted like this, because I was afraid he would have another heart attack. I would sit back while nurses and other family members tried to calm him down.

After the first month at Frazier, they tried to teach him to take a few steps with a walker, but his legs didn't move like they used to. The therapists would tell him to take baby steps, to just go a little bit at a time. With baby steps, slowly but surely, he learned to take big steps. However, none of his joints bent like they did before. The occupational therapists worked with him to pick up items with his hands from a table, but it was hard for his fingers to bend and grab things. Brushing his teeth for himself was nearly impossible.

Each time I went to visit him, I talked to him and helped him as much as I could. It was as if we were getting to know each other all over again. Sometimes I tried to help feed him his dinner. He had lost so much weight while he was in his coma. I had never seen my dad that skinny. Growing up my dad always had a mustache, but now his mustache looked bigger than his face. They made him drink Boost which was supposed to help him gain weight, but it smelled awful, and I doubt it tasted much better.

I didn't get to see my dad as much as I wanted to. Looking back on it, I think my mom attempted to keep my life as normal as possible. I had basketball practice almost every day after school. If we didn't have practice, we had a game. My mom tried to come to as many games as she could, while someone else would stay with my dad at the hospital.

One game she said she would be there, but she never showed up. The entire game I kept looking for her. It was one of those times when you know something didn't feel right, and due to recent events, I had become quite the worrier. There were a million thoughts racing through my head of what could've happened. What if something was wrong with my dad? Or what if my mom had a wreck? She promised that she would be there. Why wasn't she there?

After the game, I used one of the parent's phones to call her. I could tell something was wrong because Mom didn't sound very good. Then she told me. While she was driving to my game she had a panic attack. She was on the phone with my Aunt Jenny when suddenly everything went black. All she could do was pull over to the side of the road.

She couldn't tell my aunt where she was, only what she last remembered passing. Her mouth had drawn and she could barely speak. My aunt asked my mom what she had to eat that day. When my mom couldn't remember eating anything, Aunt Jenny told my mom that she needed to hang up and call 9-1-1, and find something to eat. There was no food in my mom's car. All she could find was a little bitty can of grape juice with a few sips left in it that I hadn't finished from that morning on our way to school. My mom called the EMS station. When Emergency Medical Services got there, they gave her fluids and found out that my mom's sugar was dangerously low. The grape juice may have been the only thing that kept anything worse from happening to her.

After she told me this story, she said that we were going to spend the night at the EMS station. She was there now. Someone from the EMS station would pick me up at the school. The paramedics and EMT's were like family. They wanted to keep an eye on her a little while longer. As soon as I got to the station, she went straight to sleep.

I stayed up almost half the night playing card games and talking about my dad. The workers there reminded me about stories of my dad and what he had been like before his heart attack. It was nice hearing everyone talk about my dad because I didn't want him to be forgotten. Even though he wasn't dead, I didn't want them to forget about all of the great things he had done before his heart attack. It was true, clinically my dad should have been dead. There was no Earthly reason that his heart was still beating. Doctors couldn't explain it. People started calling him "The Miracle Man."

The Miracle Man

A local news station, WHAS11, contacted us and wanted to do a story on my dad. Chuck Olmstead, a news anchor, was doing the story. He came to interview my dad as we were leaving Frazier Rehab. It had been almost four months since his heart attack and he was finally getting to come home. It was right before Thanksgiving. The story flashed on the television screen for a feature on the five o'clock news. Our whole town made sure their channels were set to WHAS11 that night. Mr.

Olmstead titled the segment, "The Miracle Man: a man who died and came back to life."

My dad answered all sorts of questions but he wanted to make sure the camera captured him saying, "God's up there. I saw a bright light and then I saw Him. He's real." As a nurse pushed my dad's wheelchair out the front door of the hospital and to the car, all I could think about was that the news channel was right; my dad had totally defied the odds. He showed me that you can make the impossible, possible. His story truly is a miracle. There is no other way to explain it. My dad admitted that he wasn't the one to credit for this miracle; God was the only reason he continued to win the ongoing battle.

My dad didn't go to church with us every Sunday. He didn't read his Bible every day. He wasn't a perfect man, by any means, so to hear him speak of God like that made me really pay attention. I had gone to church for as long as I could remember, but I had never given my life over to God. After everything my family had been through,

I knew that I wanted to be a follower of Christ. I wanted to be as close to Him as possible. Deep in my heart I knew that God could do anything, just like He had done for my dad. God was tugging at my heart and I felt that He had a big plan for me. Part of this plan began with my decision to give my life over to Him. My dad was known as "The Miracle Man," but I knew God was the "The Miracle Maker."

Home Sweet Home

We helped my dad as he stood up from his wheelchair and turned to get him into the passenger seat of my mom's Blazer. We buckled him up and headed home. This was the best day ever! Our house would finally feel like home again because our family would all be together.

To say my mom was driving cautiously was an understatement. She was driving like she had a newborn baby in the vehicle -- very slowly and overly careful. When we got off the interstate to head to our house, which was still twenty minutes away, countless emergency service vehicles were there to greet us and escort us through town. There were fire trucks, ambulances, police cars, sheriff vehicles, and other community members who genuinely wanted to celebrate with our family. It was like we were in a parade and my dad was the grand marshal.

Most of the vehicles accompanied us all the way to our house in Bagdad. When we pulled into our driveway, all you could see were cars parked in our yard and people anxiously awaiting our arrival. When we told my dad how many people were there, he was kind of nervous to get out of the car. He has always been the humble type and never wanted much attention. My mom, brother, and I got out of the car and walked to Dad's door; as we opened it and helped him out, all of the people started applauding. Out of nowhere our dog, 9ball, came running at my dad, full speed, trying to jump on him. Our dog had really missed my dad and had been looking for him for the past four months. 9ball jumped up and down and ran in circles all around us.

We helped my dad sit down in his wheelchair and started pushing him toward the garage. As soon as we walked through the garage doors, we saw a ramp leading into the house that was built by men from our church, in fact they had finished just before we arrived. There were lots of balloons and signs welcoming Dad home.

When we entered our home, there were many more people waiting inside to greet us. There was food everywhere in the kitchen! There was so much food that you couldn't see an inch of the countertop. Every single person must have brought us something to eat. We were beyond blessed and my dad was so happy to be home.

Having Dad at home was quite an adjustment. We had to think about ways to make our house easier for him to live in. We made lots of accommodations. We bought him a recliner with a remote that would help him stand and sit. We took down the door to the bathroom so we were able to get his wheelchair through the door. And, we attached bars on the walls to help him stand up. I will never forget the seat we had to put over top of the toilet so he could go to the bathroom. We had to get used to a lot of different things. Every time my dad wanted to get up and go to the bathroom or go to the kitchen, my mom or I helped him. At first, my mom led him everywhere. She helped him in the bathroom, the shower, and with eating.

My dad still went to outpatient physical therapy at our local hospital. His physical therapist, Phillip Herrell, really helped him come a long way. Phillip even came out to our house at night to help my dad learn his way around each room so he wouldn't need a guide. One time, he taught my dad how to dance so he could spin my mom around again. Phillip would not talk to my dad like his patient but as his friend. He didn't focus on Dad's disabilities but on his abilities to do things differently. Even though my dad was blind, had a brain injury, and was not able to do things he once could, he was still able to do a lot of things, just differently.

None of us could ever imagine how different life would be at home. I slept on the floor next to my parent's bed every night once my dad came home. I was so scared that something would happen to him again and I wanted to be there for him. Every single time I left the room, or the house, or said goodnight, I made sure to say, "I love you Dad," because I was so afraid that I wouldn't get to tell him again. If anything did happen, I wanted "I love you" to be the last thing I ever said to him, so I made sure I said it all the time.

Going Outside

My dad didn't like to go a lot of places at first, but I'll never forget the first time he went back to church. My dad, mom, brother, and I all walked into church together. As soon as we entered the sanctuary, everyone stood and clapped. We felt so loved. After his heart attack, Dad didn't like to miss church.

When we went to different places, people would look, stare, and whisper. I know they were wondering what was wrong with him or commenting that he was blind. At first, it really bothered me that people acted this way. It took me a little while to realize that Dad couldn't see people staring, and he really didn't care if they did. He was just happy to be alive and to be with his family. After I realized that my dad didn't care about what other people thought, I started trying not to care either. I got to the point where I started not noticing whether or not people were looking at us. It didn't matter to me what they thought so I just ignored everybody. When I was leading my dad around in public, I was so proud to have him holding onto my arm. I tried to focus on that. The worst part was when I forgot to tell him about a step and he fell; this happened quite a few times, but he still trusted me. I definitely had to pay more attention to wherever I was walking with him.

Not everything was easy. My dad would have his bad days. Sometimes he even felt sorry for himself. Other times he said things he didn't mean like, "Why didn't you just let me die?" Even though I don't think he realized, or at least I hope he didn't, what he was saying, it still hurt to hear him say it. Sometimes he threw tantrums because he couldn't do certain things or because we didn't ask his input on something. It was hard for him because before his heart attack, he was the decision maker and the person supporting our family. Now he was the one needing our support.

Over time, doing things on his own got a little easier. He was able to walk around our house by himself. He could give himself a shower and go to the bathroom on his own. And he learned how to feed himself. Basic things that we don't think about doing, he had to relearn. After learning how to do more and more things, he started having fewer tantrums and not feeling as sad. He learned how to fold towels, wash dishes, take out the trash, and clean up around the house. Mom would come in every once and a while, and dad would be backed in a corner, not able to move, with broken glass all around him. Those broken dishes didn't stop him because he loved doing things on his own. We got him books on tape, and he would listen to them for hours at a time. We ordered a remote with raised buttons so he could change the channels on the TV; but he mostly kept it on the same channel, TV Land.

He loved the shows on TV Land. We even put buttons on the microwave so he could "cook" for himself.

Every couple of months, he would ask to go see an eye doctor, but every single time they said the same thing, "There's nothing we can do." Some of the doctors told us that his brain might start to heal itself over time and bring back some of his vision. They tried to explain it like he was seeing out of a tiny hole, and his brain was trying to figure out what it was. We were hopeful that one day he would regain his sight. I began wishing on every single wish, birthday candle, shooting star, or clock saying 11:11 that my dad would see again. Part of me always told myself that my dad couldn't see because he had already seen Heaven. Maybe you weren't allowed to see Earth after you had seen Heaven. Maybe there was a reason why things were this way.

Our family was learning a new "normal." Eventually, we didn't think about how things "used to be."

Telling His Story

Dad never talked about dying and coming back to life. All he would tell people is "God is up there." He never explained it much more than that. This could have been because nobody ever asked him about it, or maybe he didn't feel that people would believe him.

I don't think I ever asked him because I didn't think he would want to talk about it. Our family likes to think about the future, not contemplate about our past. We don't usually talk about our feelings because we are afraid of making someone upset. No one talked about what it was like for my dad to die until one day, Dad finally told his story.

It was nearly two years since he had his heart attack, July 23, 2004. My brother was twenty years old and I was twelve. My brother had gone out with his girlfriend, and I went to a bonfire at a friend's house who lived five miles up the road. My mom was home with my dad, and they were watching their regular nightly TV shows. The subject somehow came up about the second year anniversary of Dad's heart attack being only ten days away. Dad started describing what he saw while he was dead.

At first it was hard for him to describe because he had never seen anything like it before. He shared that there was a really loud noise and he kept talking about a light. Everything just seemed really bright. Then he referenced God being there and telling him that he had a decision to make. He talked about seeing this huge thing keeping time. It looked like a clock, but it was counting down time, the time he had to make his final choice of what he wanted to do. He had two choices; stay in Heaven or come back to Earth. If he came back to Earth, he would save the lives of four children. Two of the children would be saved at Cedarmore Camp, a local site for conferences and retreats. The other two children would be saved in a car crash.

My dad talked about how hard it was for him to make the decision. He said that Heaven was so beautiful that he wanted to stay up there, but he knew God wasn't done with him on Earth. Even though he was dead for nearly an hour, he said that it felt like he was in Heaven for days. When the time came for him to make his decision, he decided to come back to Earth so God could continue to use him. He knew that he needed to help those four children that God had told him about.

Two hours after my dad told the story of what he saw in Heaven, my brother and I were hit by a drunk driver.

Earlier That Day

My friend had invited me to his house that night for a bonfire. It was my first boy/girl party. I was nervous because there was a going to be a boy there that I had a major crush on. My best friend, Bailey Coleman, and I were going together and she helped me pick out what to wear. We decided on my blue jean shorts, a cute red and white baseball tee, and flip-flops.

My mom was driving us to the party, which was five miles down the road. I don't think she was too happy when she found out that we were the only two girls there, with six other boys. All of the boys were spending the night, so there were two tents set up next to the pond -- one for the boys and one for my friend's dad, who was chaperoning.

When we got there, the boys had just returned from a hike in the woods. They decided that it would be fun to take Bailey and me on a little adventure. It didn't take long for me to realize that wearing white flip flops was not a good idea. Two hours later, we had gotten turned around and we didn't know which direction would take us back to the house. We ended up walking through soybean fields, crossing over creeks, and jumping over fences. We finally figured out where we were when we found ourselves in the neighbor's backyard. By the time we made it back to the campsite, we were starved.

We roasted hot dogs and marshmallows, and pigged out on chips and Mountain Dew. We spent the evening around the pond, fishing, telling ghost stories, and playing hide-and-go-seek in the dark. We were having lots of fun.

I talked my mom into letting me stay out until eleven o'clock that night, but I was still sad to see the headlights of a car turning back towards the field when it was time to go. Bailey's sister had come to pick us up. We tried to persuade her so we could stay a little bit longer, but she didn't fall for our tricks.

As we got ready to get into the car, we saw another pair of headlights pointing toward us. I ran to hide behind someone because I was a scaredy-cat after listening to the ghost stories. Once the car got a little closer, I saw that it was my brother in his two-door, white Honda Civic. He and his girlfriend were on their way home and decided to stop by the party. I think my mom had called and asked him to check on me.

Bailey's sister was leaving, but Bailey called her mom to see if she could spend the night with me. Her mom immediately said, "No. You need to come home with your sister, now." I stayed at the party for a little while longer with my brother. He talked to everyone there.

After nearly an hour, I was ready to leave. Mom called again to ask where we were. I climbed into the backseat of the car, and his girlfriend got into the passenger seat and waited for him to finish talking. Finally, he got in the car. The radio lit up 11:52. We were definitely late.

So Close To Home

I was muddy, sweaty, and absolutely gross. All I wanted was to go home and take a shower. We couldn't get home fast enough. Matthew's girlfriend heard me unbuckle my seatbelt and firmly reminded me to buckle up. I scooted up closer and leaned against the back of their seats. I was trying to tell her the song I wanted to listen to, "Live like You Were Dying" by Tim McGraw.

We followed a truck that was heading in the same direction as we were. Matthew thought that the driver was one of his good friends who he needed to talk to. He asked me if he should follow the truck. I never turned down a chance to spend more time with my brother, so I said I didn't care.

Moments later we passed our road. I could see our house. My mom had left the kitchen light on for us. I hoped she wouldn't be mad that we weren't home yet.

After passing our road, I can't remember what happened next. We were so close to home, less than a mile away.

I know it wasn't my fault, but I always think about how I'm the reason we were in that exact spot at two minutes till midnight. If I had not gone to the bonfire, then Matthew would not have had to come pick me up. If I had not told Matthew that it was okay to follow that truck, then we would have gone straight home. Maybe it never would have happened.

Other People Telling My Story

I force myself to try and remember what happened that night, but I have to rely on what other people tell me about it. I've asked questions of everyone involved to try to remember more about that night. I've written down what they have told me. While people tell their stories, they refer to me as Kelly or the young girl. I'm glad to hear other people tell my story so I have something to remember.

My Brother's Memory.

*My brother remembers everything about that night.
He tells me that he's happy that I don't remember.
If I could, I would take the memories away from
him, too. From the time I was a little girl, I've
always been on his heels, following closely behind
him; he's someone I always wanted to be like. He's
taught me so much, and I've given him so little in
return. He helped save my life. My brother,
Matthew Burgin, will always and forever be my role
model.*

"I had gone to Louisville to eat dinner with my
girlfriend. After we ate, we came back to
Shelbyville, stopped at a gas station, and
continued home toward Bagdad. It was nearly
11:00 p.m. when we went to pick up Kelly. The
kids were all sitting around the campfire, talking
and roasting marshmallows, so we joined in.

My mom had already called me twice to
ask where I was and when I was coming home,
and Kelly was pestering me to leave. My

girlfriend, Kelly, and I finally left the bonfire at ten minutes till midnight and headed toward home. Once we turned onto Bagdad Road, I saw a friend of mine driving a truck in front of us. I had been meaning to talk to him, so I followed the truck. It ended up not being my friend.

I remember following the truck going up a little hill, and a car came around the curve really fast. It swerved into our lane—then the other lane— and then back into our lane, over the line, everywhere. He swerved to miss the truck in front of us, and he went off the side of the road. Then he came back up, correcting himself to get off the side of the road, and cut straight in front of us. We T-boned. I hit the car in its side. I couldn't stop. I tried to hit the brakes, but it all happened so fast. There was nothing I could do. He was coming over that hill, so were we—it was just split seconds.

When the impact occurred it spun the back of our car to the left. It jerked us, and the passenger side of his car hit the front of mine and caused the rear of my car to fling to the left. The front of my car folded up, and I couldn't see out the windshield.

Once the airbags deployed, it took me a second to see if this was real.

Kelly had propelled between the two front seats, her head went through the windshield, and her back was facing me. I couldn't help but think she was dead. My girlfriend was in the passenger seat, unconscious. I was the only one in the car alert. I started talking to both of them to see if I get could get any form of response. My girlfriend started screaming and acting frantic, as if she didn't know where she was. Kelly didn't respond. Finally, Kelly made a noise -- a moaning sound. She wasn't really saying anything. Several bystanders came to help and called 9-1-1.

I opened my door and tried to get out. I couldn't. My legs wouldn't move. I had to pick up my legs and set them outside the car; they just folded under me. My knees collapsed, and my legs were like jello. All I could do was sit there and try to work with Kelly.

I just wanted her to talk to me, to say something. I tried to hold Kelly up. I put her hip on my shoulder to keep her spine in line until help arrived. While I was holding her, she started screaming. Her scream was piercing. I couldn't get her to calm down. When she stopped screaming, I tried to get her to talk to me, but she kept drifting in and out of consciousness. It didn't even look like Kelly. That girl in the windshield didn't look at all like my sister."

Jimmy Baxter: First on the Scene.
Jimmy Baxter was a stranger to me before that night. He was the one driving the truck in front of us that my brother thought was his friend. He lived a mile from my house, but I never knew his name. After that night, he became a person I will always

think highly of because he turned around and came
back to help us.

"I'll never forget that night. I was on my way home. I've had incidents in the past that have caused me to be an extra cautious driver. When I looked into my rearview mirror, I saw a car turn off Trammel Road and start to follow me. The car wasn't riding my bumper but was close enough to keep my attention. Not even half a mile past FrysOldburg Road, a car coming toward me from the opposite direction nearly hit me; it was out of control. It was scary. At the last minute, the car swerved and missed me only by a hair. I saw the car go off toward the ditch but I couldn't see anything once I started down the hill and around the curve. I kept looking into my rearview mirror, thinking that the car following me should be popping over the hill right behind me. When I didn't see the car's headlights come over the hill, I knew something bad had happened.

I turned around in the closest driveway and headed back. As soon as I popped over the hill, I saw the worst thing I've ever seen. I pulled off on the side of the road. There were two cars; one was white and the other teal. Both of the doors were closed on the teal car, and I recognized it instantly as the car that nearly hit me. When I looked over to the white car, the driver's door was open. I started running toward it, but knew I had to stay calm.

There were three people in the white car. A guy, who looked to be in his twenties, was in the driver's seat. A girl, about the same age, was in the passenger seat. Finally, there was a younger girl whose face had gone through the windshield. It looked like the guy in the driver's seat was trying to get out of the car, but his legs were like rubber; he couldn't move.

The younger girl in the windshield . . . I thought she was dead. Her body was limp and looked completely lifeless. She wasn't moving and wasn't saying anything. After a few minutes, she started to make faint groans every now and then, but that was it. Her brother kept trying to talk to her, trying to get her to respond.

The other girl in the passenger seat was completely hysterical. She was flinging her arms everywhere. I was afraid she was going to hurt the little girl in the windshield. The guy in the driver's seat kept shouting, 'Get her out of the car! Get her out of the car!'

Another man drove up on the wreck and walked toward the car; I didn't get the other man's name. He started helping me peel back the glass of the passenger door on the white car. The glass had shattered, but it was still hard to pull back. We were able to get the hysterical girl in the passenger seat out through the passenger window and set her in the grass beside the car.

Then I went over to the teal car. Now the driver's door was open. There was a man lying on the ground beside the car; he was trying to move around but couldn't. When I looked inside the teal car, there was a woman in the passenger seat, but she was. . . she was dead.

I got out my phone to call 9-1-1. I started getting frustrated because the call wouldn't go through. After my third try, I gave up. I called my wife and briefly told her what was going on and where I was, and I asked her if she would call 9-1-1.

It wasn't long after that when other people started arriving on the scene. It was only a few minutes until first responders, volunteer firefighters, paramedics, and police officers surrounded both cars, attending to the five people involved in the crash. I just stepped away and stood off to the side. I thought the best thing I could do was stay out of the way."

Christine Quire: Before the Ambulance.

Christine Quire has been a part of my life since I was a baby. Her house is only 1.6 miles away from mine. Her daughter used to babysit me. When I was in elementary school, she was the lunch lady. She always called me "Lucky."

"I was freezing corn that night with Rick, my husband. My daughter Karol called and said, 'Mom, Matt and Kelly have been in a wreck down the street. I need you to come down here now!' So I took off and went to the scene.

I pulled off the side of the road and ran straight to Matthew's car. All I could hear was Kelly screaming; the sound was piercing. Matt kept saying over and over again, 'It's going to be okay, Kelly. Everything's going to be okay. Don't be upset. Don't cry, Kelly. Christine, please take care of Kelly.'

I stood there not knowing what to do. Matt had blood pouring down his face. He said, 'Christine, go get me something so I can put it over this cut on my forehead.'

I snapped back at him, 'Get out of the car.' At this point, I didn't know that his legs were broken and he couldn't move. Matt's legs were positioned outside of the car; I guess he had lifted and placed them there. Kelly was thrown over top of the center console. The other girl in the car didn't say a whole lot to me.

The ambulances were coming and it seemed like forever, but I could hear them coming. I turned and I looked for someone to give me something that Matt could put on his forehead. A first responder handed me a pair of gloves. I went straight over and stuck the gloves on Matt's forehead to try and stop the bleeding. Matt just said, 'What am I supposed to do with these gloves on my forehead?' I didn't realize that the first responder had given me the gloves to put on MY hands!

By this time, the ambulance had finally arrived. I am pretty sure someone else walked over with gauze or something to put over Matt's cut. Everyone was talking around me. There was so much going on, but it was hard to hear anything because of Kelly's screams. They were trying to pull the glass back from the windshield to get Kelly out. I heard someone say that the helicopter was coming. They kept talking about needing two separate helicopters -- one for Matt and one for Kelly. Matt said, 'I'm not going without Kelly. We'll go in the same helicopter.'

I volunteered to get Matt and Kelly's parents, Jack and Michelle, because I thought I could help a lot more that way."

Waldo: Paramedic at the Scene.

"Waldo," a nickname for Brandon Berry, was one of my brother's best friends growing up. When they graduated high school, Waldo became a paramedic for Shelby County, and my brother went to college. The two stayed in touch, keeping up with each other, even after high school.

"I was working as a paramedic for Shelby County at Station 1. That night I was working with Scott Anderson, Shawn Doty, and Jarrod Sights. They dispatched it as a head-on collision on Bagdad Road, so all four of us headed that way. As we got closer, we kept listening to the scanner. We heard that there were two possible dead people and several injuries.

When we pulled up on the scene, I remember seeing someone lodged in the windshield of the white car, but I didn't recognize who it was. I went around to the driver's side of the car and saw Matt. I remember asking Matt, 'Whose head is in the windshield?' He told me, 'It's Kelly.'

There were a few people on the scene huddled around, holding Kelly's head and neck in place, trying to keep her from moving so she didn't cut herself even more. I couldn't believe it was Kelly; her face was completely swollen and covered with blood. I remember helping Matt and his girlfriend.

I looked over and saw the other paramedics taking William Henson, the driver of the teal car, out of the ditch. They put him onto a stretcher, and then into the ambulance. Henson was cussing and carrying on — a typical drunk person. I worked to put Matt's girlfriend on a stretcher and into the same ambulance as William Henson. Once they were loaded, the ambulance left quickly and headed for Jewish Hospital Shelbyville.

I overheard someone calling for a helicopter. I'm not sure who the helicopter was intended for, but I'm pretty sure it was for Kelly because of her severe head injury. It could have been for Matt because he had lost so much blood and had two broken legs. I found out that it was coming for both Kelly and Matt.

Kelly was combative. She was fighting. Once the helicopter got there, they didn't want to take Kelly because she was so hysterical. Matthew said that he wasn't going on the helicopter unless Kelly went with him. Matt stayed calm the whole time. He said that he was in no pain, but he was only worried about Kelly. He kept trying to keep Kelly calm. We asked if we tied Kelly's hands and legs down, would they take her on the helicopter. They agreed. That's exactly what we did. We put tape over top of Kelly's head and fixed straps across her arms, chest, and legs so she was completely restrained.

We flew Kelly and Matt out from the field next to their house. They took Kelly to Kosair Children's Hospital and Matt to U of L Hospital. After the helicopter took off, I got back into the ambulance and drove back to the scene. That's when I walked over to the teal car. I saw Tammy, the woman who died. She had been the passenger in the teal car. She was pretty much on the driver's side, because the passenger and driver's seat were nearly pushed together. It all happened so fast."

My Brother's Memory after Help Arrived.

"Once the EMS and Fire Department arrived, they got me out of the car. They had to get me out quickly so they could get to Kelly. They placed me on a spine board, on a stretcher, and in a neck brace. They put me into an ambulance where they took my vitals, put an IV in my arm, and made sure I was stabilized. I had lost a lot of blood.

I kept looking up to see what they were doing with Kelly, but I couldn't see her. Once they got Kelly out, they put her in the ambulance with me. They were flying us in a helicopter to stat flight us to Louisville. At first, they didn't want to take Kelly. By this time, she was pretty combative, but there was no way I was going without her. They decided to take her on the helicopter only if she was restrained. That's exactly what they did: they tied her hands and feet down.

I could see our house when they loaded me into the helicopter. We were so close to home. Once they got us both into the helicopter, we were gone. I tried talking to Kelly the entire time we were in the air. I couldn't get her to calm down, and she wouldn't lie still. They dropped Kelly off first at Kosair Children's Hospital and then went back into the air to take me to University Hospital."

Christine Left the Scene to Tell My Parents.

"Before I went to tell Jack and Michelle about what happened to their kids, I went back to my house and got Rick, my husband. There was no way I was going to go tell them by myself. We had to go around the back road because the main road was blocked off from the wreck.

When we got to the house, Rick and I walked straight through the back door; luckily it was unlocked. Rick kept calling, 'Jack, Jack, Jack, wake up!' Kelly's mom flew from the bedroom saying, 'What's wrong? Christine, what's wrong? Where are my kids?'

I knew that she had already heard the helicopter fly over top of the house, so she had put it all together. I tried to calmly explain, 'Kelly and Matt have been in a wreck, but everything's going to be okay. They're going to be okay.' Honestly, I didn't know if everything was going to be okay, but there is no way I could tell Jack and Michelle that.

Rick helped Jack get ready, and we left for the hospital. As we were running out the door, Kelly's mom turned back to get Molly, Kelly's doll. She couldn't be without it. We got into the car, but when we got to the end of the road, we were stopped. Workers were trying to get the ambulance through to get Matt and Kelly to the helicopter. Before I had time to say anything, Jack was out of the car and walking around toward the front. It took everything I had to keep Michelle in the car. Thankfully, there was someone there to stop Jack and tell him that he needed to get back in the car and go to the hospital. Michelle was holding Molly outside the window saying, 'Kelly needs her doll, Molly! Please take Molly to Kelly! She'll be scared without her doll!' One of the paramedics took Molly from Michelle and ran it to Kelly. They were in the field being loaded into the helicopter.

We sat in the car and watched as the helicopter lifted. Once we couldn't see the helicopter anymore, we took off, and I drove as fast as I could to get Michelle and Jack to the hospital."

My Dad Heard the News.

My dad may have a brain injury and not able to remember a lot of things, but this was a night he would never forget.

"I remember Rick and Christine Quire coming back into the bedroom and waking me. I was in my drawers when he said, 'Get up, Jack.' I shot out of bed. I remember hearing the helicopter flying over the house. I knew it was bad.

We got into Christine's car. When we got to the end of our road, one of the paramedics came over to the car and said, 'We're taking them to Louisville in the helicopter.' He wouldn't answer any more questions but said that it was pretty bad. Christine drove to the hospital fast. It didn't take long to get there, but it sure felt like a long time. When we arrived and they let us see Kelly, I sat by her and held her hand. All I did *was sit by her bed and told her that everything would be okay, while I listened to her moan."*

Kelly

I didn't know I was in a helicopter. I didn't know
the people who were talking to me. I didn't know
where I was, where I was going, or why they
wouldn't let me move. People tried to tell me what
was going on. They asked me so many questions
that I couldn't answer.

My Aunt Jenny and Uncle Scott were the
first ones to get to the hospital with me. When they
got there, I was getting X-ray's, MRI's, and a CAT
scan. Everyone told my family that they were
concerned about a brain injury and possible
blindness in my left eye. Nothing was certain, but
they told my family to be prepared for the worst.
The nurse warned my aunt and uncle that I didn't
look like myself.

My aunt told me that when she first saw me I was thrashing and wouldn't sit still. The nurses tried to talk to me and told me to lie still so they could run scans. I was screaming and saying all kinds of stuff. "Bailey, get that hot dog off my face! I love you Aunt Jenny! I love you." Then I started singing Tim McGraw's song, "I went sky diving. I went rocky mountain climbing . . . And someday I hope you get the chance to live like you were dying." I guess it was pretty ironic to be belting out these words in the Emergency Room. I was hysterical.

All of a sudden, I stopped moving and it was hard to breathe. When I tried taking a breath, it only made it worse. I couldn't move my head forward to get any air because I was strapped down. In one motion, vomit came out of my mouth and went all over me and the CAT scan machine. Blood shot straight up like a missile from the gash on my forehead. Everyone started freaking out, especially my aunt; they tried to get me out of the machine. As soon as I vomited, then it and the blood came straight back on to me. I wasn't able to get all of the puke out of my throat since I was lying on my back, tied down, so I was starting to gurgle. They had to get my head out and turned to the side so I wouldn't choke on my own vomit.

That CAT scan machine was temporarily closed. I was moved down the hall to a different location. This night was never going to end. The medical staff gave me pain medication and medicine to keep me calm, but they wouldn't let me sleep. Since I had a head injury and a concussion, the doctors wanted to keep me awake. I think they were afraid that if I went to sleep, I may not wake up.

My mom and dad finally got there and came into the room with me. They said that there were a lot more people in the waiting room. Every time I started to doze off, someone would say my name and ask me questions. I didn't feel well. I just remember everyone around me saying, "Everything's going to be okay." I knew they were just saying that. No one, including me, really believed it.

Matthew

Once I got to the Emergency Room, nurses and doctors rushed around me. I had lost so much blood in the wreck that they quickly started a transfusion. It felt so weird watching someone else's blood being pumped into my body. They gave me medication and I started to feel a little groggy. Everyone around me was saying so much that it was hard to keep up. I searched for a familiar face to ask how Kelly was doing.

It felt so surreal that we had been in a wreck. I didn't understand why the car was turned sideways in the road. I felt like what happened was all my fault. I wish I could go back and take us home instead of following that truck. We were so close to our house; I tried to be strong and brave, so I didn't tell anyone that I was scared. Deep down, I was afraid that I would never walk again.

I got to see Mom and Dad briefly before I was sent to get X-rays and MRIs. They had been told that Kelly and I were going to be at the same hospital. Once they found out that she was at the children's hospital, I told them to go be with her. She was so little and there were other family members coming to be with me.

After the tests, the doctors were able to see that almost every single bone in each of my legs was broken. My legs were crushed on impact. They decided to put external fixators on both of my legs. This was to keep my legs stabilized until they could do surgery and put rods into them. I had to be sedated while they put the external fixators on, but when I saw them for the first time, my legs looked like a robot. All that held my legs together was the metal attached to them.

The medical staff moved someone into the bed beside me in the Emergency Room. A family member found out that it was William Henson, the driver of the other vehicle in the crash. I overheard limited conversations back and forth between our two families, mostly trying to figure out what had happened in the wreck. I found out that William Henson was drunk; he had gotten behind the wheel under the influence of alcohol and tried to drive home.

This crash happened because a drunk driver was thoughtless enough to get behind the wheel and put everyone's life, not only his, in danger. I was furious!

We also found out that the drunk driver's girlfriend, who was in the passenger side of his vehicle, didn't make it. I remember seeing her at the crash. I knew she wouldn't make it when I saw her. Our car hit directly into the passenger side. Tests revealed that both

William Henson and his girlfriend had blood alcohol levels three times the legal limit.

Knowing the reason for the crash didn't help me handle all that I felt. I was so mad at that guy lying in the hospital bed next to me. At the same time, I felt sorry for the woman who died and for her family. We later found out that she had two kids. I hated thinking that those kids would grow up without knowing their mom. Even though the crash wasn't my fault, all I could think about was that my car had hit her.

While lying in that hospital bed, completely still, I knew my entire life was changed forever. The decision that drunk driver made that night would forever change my life, Kelly's life, and our entire family's lives. I really hoped and prayed that Kelly would be okay. I couldn't live with myself if anything happened to her.

Kelly

My head felt like it had been slammed against a brick wall. There was so much pressure built up in my face that it felt like it was going to explode. It was itching so badly, but every time I tried to scratch it, my mom would swipe my hand away.

It was impossible to see out of my left eye, so I had to turn my head to see anyone in the room. Different people came in and out of my room all day, but it was nearly impossible for me to talk to them. I could hardly keep my eyes open and stay awake, but I could overhear my mom talking to some of our friends who had come to see me. She was talking about me. Thankfully, she said, the doctors had found no sign of brain injury but they did not want to say that as a definite. The doctors weren't sure about the eyesight in my left eye. They had to wait until the swelling went down to be able to tell anything. My sinus cavities on the left side of my face were crushed, and the orbital bone around my eye was broken. The plastic surgeons discussed if surgery was necessary to reset the break. It was a waiting game until we would know anything. The lacerations on my forehead, cheek, neck, and shoulder were severe. I still had a lot of glass that needed to be removed. No one said a word to me about how my brother was doing. Even when I asked about him, I was ignored as if I hadn't asked a question.

Later that day, a group of nurses walked in carrying a tray full of shiny utensils. They laid it right next to my bed. One of the nurses put pain medication into my IV. Even though they told me not to look, it was still hard not to notice the amount of hardware sitting beside me. Moments later, they used it to pick pieces of glass out of my face. The worst was when they took a wire brush and scrubbed it over the top of my forehead to get out all the little smithereens of glass.

After they cleaned my face, neck, and shoulders, the nurses tried straightening my hair, which was knotted with blood and glass. One of the nurses took an electric razor and started buzzing off my hair. They began at the front of my forehead and took a huge chunk of hair off the right side. My family watched, mortified.

My Aunt Kathy jumped up and asked the nurses what they were doing. They explained that there was no way they could get all of the glass and blood out of my hair. They would try to save as much hair as they could. She responded, "We will clean Kelly's hair out. You are not cutting any more of it off." The nurses didn't say much but quickly exited the room, leaving my aunt to clean my hair.

***

I knew that I looked awful. When visitors entered the room, they almost took a step back in shock when they saw me. Everyone who came in tried to hide their initial expression, but I wanted to know what I looked like. Days passed, and I asked my mom if I could see myself. Each time she said no.

I remember lying in the hospital bed with a bunch of visitors in my room. Someone brought me balloons and sat them on the tray table next to my bed. I kept asking for someone to turn the balloon around so I could see the other side. My mom caught on to what I was trying to do. The back side of the balloon was shiny and reflective; I was trying to see myself! I almost got them to turn the balloon completely around when my mom stopped them.

The next time she caught me trying to see myself, I was in the small bathroom in my room. There was only a toilet inside, no shower or mirror. I still needed a lot of help walking around, especially with all the cords attached to me, so my mom walked with me to the bathroom. She stood outside the door and waited for me. After a few minutes, she peaked in and caught me staring at the silver toilet paper holder. I was moving my head around, trying to catch a glimpse of my face.

Finally, she asked if I wanted to see myself. I said yes.

She walked me from the bathroom to the sink and mirror near the door. I remember walking to the mirror, with my mom by my side, and turning to see myself. I can't remember what I saw in the mirror after I turned. It's like my mind blocked the image from my memory. My mom told me that I stared at myself for a few seconds and then just turned back to the bed, not saying a word. To this day I have no clue what I looked like then. My mom wouldn't let anyone take pictures of me for months after the crash. She didn't want me to have to remember myself looking like that.

Matthew

My first surgery was the day after the wreck. I would have a series of surgeries over the next couple of weeks to try to piece my legs back together. The doctors were hopeful. I tried to stay optimistic, especially for my family's sake. I didn't want to complain too much about my legs hurting.

Everyone gave me updates on Kelly. The news was vague but it always sounded positive. I had someone buy a little stuffed dog from the gift shop and take it over to her from me. They said she would probably be in the hospital for a week before she could go home. I wanted to see her again, but I didn't know if I could handle it. I really felt like I let her down.

My entire family was so supportive. Someone was constantly with me at the hospital. My grandparents, aunts, and uncles all took turns spending the night with me. I couldn't get out of my bed; my legs weren't able to hold me up. I had to lie down twenty-four hours a day. So, having family with me was really helpful.

Every couple of days, I had another surgery. They would put another rod into my leg or a screw into my ankle. There were only about three inches of my left leg that didn't need some kind of surgery on it. It seemed like the operations were endless.

Even though all I could do was lie flat on my back, I tried to think as little as possible. Every single time I started thinking about what happened, I started to become depressed about Kelly, mad about the drunk driver, and concerned about what would happen with my life. There was no way I was going to return to college in August. I was supposed to start my junior year. I wasn't only worried about college but mostly if I would be able to walk again. I loved playing softball and basketball, but now I wasn't even sure if I would be able to walk, let alone run. Trying not to think was the best option with all of these things to worry about.

My goal for each day was to make it through the day and focus on the little accomplishments. After two weeks, I was allowed to stand up beside the bed for the first time. I held onto a support, and I only stood for a few seconds, but I put weight on my legs! We were excited about the little things I was starting to do again. Each day I tried to stand a little longer or move my legs a little more.

The doctors said they would send me to a rehabilitation hospital in a few weeks. I needed to rebuild the muscles in my legs and to relearn how to walk. Part of me felt embarrassed that I was twenty years old and had to learn how to walk again. But it gave me something to work toward.

I would still have to come back for more surgeries. The doctors estimated that there would be a total of ten surgeries on my legs. I was still near the starting line on a long road to recovery. Realistically, I knew that both Kelly and I would have a lot to deal with emotionally, physically, and mentally. We had to process the crash and learn to cope with what happened.

Our family has always dealt with things differently; we've never been able to talk about our feelings with one another. So, I was a little anxious for the day I would see Kelly again. I had no clue what I would say. I didn't know if I was supposed to tell her that I was sorry. I didn't want to ask her the cliché questions that everyone asked about how she was doing. Maybe she would be mad at me because of what happened. Maybe she blamed me. I prayed God would give me the words to say and the strength to get through it when I did see her.

A lot of people prayed for me, Kelly, and our family. People sent balloons, flowers, stuffed animals, and cards. As much pain as I felt, I couldn't help but feel blessed to know that there were so many people who cared and were rooting for me to finish the race, even if they had to pick me up and carry me.

Kelly

I spent nearly a week in the hospital. The doctors ran all of the tests possible and there was nothing else they could do. My swelling did not go away, but they believed I would have full vision when it did. They saw no indication of any permanent brain injury. It was just going to take time for the wounds to heal.

I received a lot of rules before the doctors would discharge me from the hospital. I wasn't allowed to have any physical activity, at least until I came back for a check-up. I had to put antibacterial ointment on my face three times a day. I wasn't supposed to start back to school in August. There was an endless list of precautions for me to take, including not playing basketball.

When I heard this, the tears started pouring down my cheeks. I didn't want to miss my first day of school for eighth grade. I especially didn't want to miss my eighth grade year of basketball. After many debates and deliberations, it was decided that I could go to school for partial days in the beginning of the year, though it was not recommended. Also, it was strongly suggested that I wait a while before trying basketball. I would need to wear a face mask when I finally did play.

I wasn't mad about being extra cautious. I knew that things had changed completely, but I just didn't understand why. What did I do to deserve this? Why did my family have to suffer through another tragedy?

After my dad's heart attack I explained it to myself by thinking that God allowed it to happen so we could be closer as a family. My dad and I did grow closer to Him. But now, two years later, was the devil testing us? Was the devil angry and tempting me because I had grown so much closer to

God? I couldn't explain anything. I couldn't answer these questions. Maybe it was my fault, after all.

***

The ride home from the hospital was horrible. My parents didn't let me see my brother before I went home. They said they wanted me to go home and get some rest. But I knew it was because they didn't want my brother to see me. The wreck was not his fault at all, but my brother felt guilty because of what had happened to his little sister. He felt as if he was responsible for me and had let me down. He thought that he should have been able to protect me at the time of the crash. Everyone worried that if he saw me, it would make him upset and make his recovery more difficult.

I puked on the way home. Then when I got home, I puked again. Over the next few days I couldn't stop throwing up. Nothing stayed in my stomach, and I became dehydrated. My mom went and stayed with my brother at the hospital every day. My dad stayed home with me. My mom asked family members or other close friends to stay with us. At first, she wasn't worried about me getting sick, but after a few days she took me back to the hospital.

They ran more tests and readmitted me into the hospital. My sodium and potassium levels were dangerously low, and there was concern about me possibly having a seizure. I had to stay in the hospital so they could keep an eye on me. I didn't know I was going to stay, so I didn't have Molly, my favorite doll.

I was placed on a different floor at Kosair, in an area that used to be reserved for tuberculosis patients. One of the walls had arm sleeves where the nurses and doctors used to reach in to tend to the quarantined patients. It was kind of creepy, especially because my hospital bed was right against this particular, strange wall. Every couple of hours a nurse came in to check my blood levels and see how I was doing. I had to get my potassium and sodium to normal levels and have them stay consistent before I was allowed to go back home.

I remained at Kosair for another week. This time, I was more alert and mobile, so I complained about being bored. During the first few days I was there, my mom took me down to the gift shop. I found something that I just had to have: a Snoopy and Charlie Brown coloring book. My mom let me buy it, along with a pack of crayons. I found my new favorite hobby. When I was awake, I was coloring in that coloring book. I hated it when I had to stop and let the nurses take my blood or when I had to eat. I was so meticulous in coloring every single page. I would get elaborate with shading and outlining. I loved coloring.

I didn't realize it, but I had found a way to cope with all that was happening. I reverted to being a child, a time when things were simpler and bad stuff didn't seem to happen. Coloring was my escape, and it made everything seem okay.

Also, during this week, I developed a new, annoying habit: the sniffles. The bones in my face were broken and my sinus cavities were crushed. Most of the time, I felt like I couldn't breathe. So, I would sniffle like someone who had a cold -- except I did not have a cold. I would sniffle all of the time. It got on everyone's nerves, but I couldn't help it.

After a week passed and I had been fully poked and prodded, the doctors told me that it was finally safe for me to go home. They could never explain why my levels were all messed up. They could only explain it as a result of my body suffering through a traumatic experience. I had to drink lots of Gatorade and stay hydrated after I went home. I was so happy to be going home again.

This time, my mom and dad were going to let me see my big brother. I had colored him a picture and wrote a get well soon note at the bottom. The picture I chose was of Snoopy and Woodstock because they were best buds, just like me and my brother. I was so nervous to see him but excited at the same time. I wondered what he was thinking about seeing me or if he even knew I was coming. I had no clue what I was going to say. I held on to my picture super tight as we walked into the hospital and stepped onto the elevator.

Matthew Sees Kelly

I didn't know Kelly was coming to see me until she and my parents were on their way up in the elevator. When she walked into the room, following closely behind my parents, I tried hard not to look her straight in the eye. I still had a guilty conscience; I felt like I had done this to her.

Kelly's face was red. Scabs had started to form across her forehead and on the side of her right cheek. She wore a pink baseball cap but it didn't hide all of the scratches. Her face was swollen, mostly on the left side. She couldn't open her left eye all the way. Even though she was bruised and scarred, I couldn't help but grin when I saw her. My little sister was here, and she looked absolutely beautiful to me.

As Kelly walked into the room, holding on tightly to her doll, Molly, she was a little hesitant about what to do or where to go. There were a few other visitors in the room, so she walked in slowly looking toward the floor. Then she walked over to my hospital bed and threw her arms around me. She gave me the biggest hug and proudly handed me the picture she had colored. My eyes teared up as I read the sweet note she had written at the bottom of the page. I handed the picture to my grandmother so she could put it up in the window.

Kelly found a chair near a corner and sat down. I think she was trying not to look at my legs. I didn't know what my parents had told her about me, but I'm sure it was scary for her to see those fixators attached to the outside of my legs. We didn't say much to each other. Also, we tried our best not to look at each other for more than a second at a time. It was awkward. I wanted to say I was sorry, but I didn't think this was the right time, especially with all the other people around. I wanted to ask her how she felt, but I was afraid of her answer. I'm sure that's all she had been asked for the past two weeks. That's all people were asking me.

My parents explained that they were taking Kelly back home. They didn't stay long. Mom promised she would be back the next day unless Kelly needed her at home. My grandparents were going to stay the night with me again. I was so happy Kelly was going home, but I was also a little jealous. I didn't know how long it would be until I got to do the same thing. I tried to stay optimistic, especially in front of Kelly.

Right before they left, Kelly walked over to me. I thought she was coming to give me a hug, but she bent over a little closer and whispered, "Does it hurt?"

I knew she was talking about my legs. I also knew that she didn't need to know that it was the worst pain I have felt in my entire life. So, I looked her straight in the eyes and said, "No, it doesn't hurt at all. I'll be home with you and walking around in no time." She nodded her head and turned toward the door. I watched as she left the room and headed down the hallway. All I could think about was how I would never have a clue what she was going through or what she would face. All I could do was be there for her along the way.

Kelly Sees Matthew

Walking into Matthew's hospital room was terrifying. I think it was worse because my parents had tried to keep me away from him. It made me more nervous to finally see him.

I let my parents walk into the room first. There were so many other people in the room, it made me hesitant to go in. I didn't know others would be there. I felt like they were staring at me, mostly at my face. I knew everyone was thinking that I looked funny, so I just tried to look at the floor.

As soon as I saw Matthew in the hospital bed, I ran over to give him a hug. I presented the surprise coloring page that I had colored for him. Then I sat down in the chair closest to the door, trying to hide my face. Matthew had huge bars attached to his legs. They looked like something you would see attached to a robot. His face looked pale. He had a cut on his forehead, too, but his wasn't as big as mine.

There were so many questions racing through my head that I wanted to ask Matthew. I wanted to know what surgeries he had, if his legs hurt, and when he was coming home from the hospital. I also wondered if he remembered what had happened, because I couldn't. I had been trying so hard to remember what had happened to us after we left the bonfire. I just couldn't.

While I was sitting there, it was hard to pay attention to what others around me were saying. Some people tried to ask me questions about how I was doing, but I just told them I was okay. I didn't tell them how I really felt. Mostly, I was confused.

There seemed to be so much that people weren't telling me and so much that had happened that I didn't know. At the same time, I didn't know if I wanted to know. I wondered why Matthew wasn't saying anything to me. Maybe he was thinking the same things I was thinking. Maybe he was scared, just like me.

I was just ready to go home, and I was ready for my big brother to be home with me.

Coloring
A New
Page

When my parents and I got home, things were not the same as before the wreck. My parents seemed to walk on eggshells around me, making sure they didn't do or say things that would make me upset. They treated me differently. I know they were trying to protect and support me, but I felt like I was in a bubble. This was another time when life at our house changed.

During the day, different people came and sat with me while Mom went to the hospital to be with my brother. I just sat around and colored, page after page, day after day. My goal was to get the entire coloring book finished. Some of my friends came to visit me sometimes, but there wasn't a lot for us to do together. I wasn't allowed to do any physical activity, so we just sat around and watched movies.

I slept by my parents' bed every night. I was afraid to be alone. My mom spread out a stack of blankets for me to lie on next to her side of the bed. It was embarrassing that I was almost thirteen years old and I was sleeping in my parents' bedroom, but I couldn't sleep in my room. When I tried to sleep in my bed, bad thoughts poured into my head, and I couldn't stay still. Neither of my parents ever got angry when I woke them up in the middle of the night after my nightmares. Sometimes I would wake up screaming, and other times I would wake up while trying to scream but couldn't. I would open my mouth and nothing came out.

***

There were two weeks left of summer vacation before I was supposed to start the eighth grade. The doctors recommended that I not go back to school immediately, but I wanted to go back so badly. Most kids would probably be more than excited if they didn't have to go back to school, but not me. I wanted something to finally feel normal. Going back to school would seem like things were the same as before the wreck.

My mom went to the school to talk about my coming back and my special circumstances. I was supposed to be in gym class, but my mom asked if they could switch my schedule since I wasn't allowed to have any physical activity. My mom also got special permission for me to wear a hat at school. Hats could be worn only on certain days, but they would let me wear mine all of the time. I wanted to wear a hat to try to hide my scabs. They were starting to look gross, and I had to put an antibiotic ointment on my face three times a day. The school was prepared for my return, but my mom didn't tell them when that would be.

It took two weeks for me to convince my mom to let me start back to school with everyone else on the first day. We compromised. I would start with just three hours on the first day. I wore a brand new outfit -- a pink button-up shirt with blue jeans, wedges, and my baseball cap. My mom drove Bailey and me to school that morning. Bailey's dad would pick me up halfway through the day.

No one said a lot on the car ride to school. I was really nervous. Bailey told me not to worry about anything; she would walk in and sit beside me in the bleachers. She also said she would beat up anyone who said anything bad to me. I really hoped that didn't happen because I knew she was being honest. She would've punched anyone in the face if they made fun of me.

Walking into the school was intimidating. All of the teachers were there when we walked in the front door. Most of them greeted me with hugs and said they were surprised to see me. Many asked how I was doing. My answers to their questions were brief. I kept walking toward the gym, which is where students gathered in the mornings. Some of my friends ran up and told me I looked pretty. I knew they were just trying to be nice.

We waited on the bleachers until the teachers came in. Our entire eighth grade class went outside to huddle up on the hill and listen for our name to be called. Our first period teacher would call our names and we would follow him or her to the classroom.

Teacher after teacher came up, but I didn't hear my name. All of my friends were called, and I hoped that I would be in classes with some of them. Finally, the last teacher came up and went through her roster. I thought I would be in this last group, but my name was not called. I am sure there was a rational reason why I wasn't called, but I was more emotional than usual. I fought back tears. As my friends started walking toward their classrooms, I didn't know where to go. I just stood there looking down at the ground. I shouldn't have come back to school yet.

One of the eighth grade teachers, Mrs. Black, came up and took me by the arm. I'm sure she could tell that I was about to melt into a puddle. She said she knew what had happened. I followed her to the main office where she informed me that they had taken me out of the computer scheduling system. They didn't know when I would start back to school and did not want the days I was absent to count against me. The ladies in the office had saved my intended schedule and knew exactly where to direct me.

As I walked into my first period classroom, all of my friends were there. I was glad to see familiar faces. The only bad part was that the one seat left in the room was in the center of the front row. This may have been a good thing. My back was to everyone else, and I couldn't see whether or not they were looking at my scabby face.

The first day went by so fast. In my third class I was called to the main office to leave. I was exhausted. It was a good thing that I had planned for a half-day because I was worn out after only three hours of classes.

As much as I wanted everything to feel the same at school, it didn't. I expected everyone to look at me funny so I tried to prepare myself. Still, it didn't feel good to catch people staring. I felt like an outcast. My friends were being nice to me, but it felt like they were trying hard to be nice. They were acting like my parents, walking on eggshells around me. A few of my friends were stand-offish; they didn't know how they should act around me. I'm sure I irritated a lot of people, especially because I had developed these annoying sniffles with my sinus cavities crushed. I felt like I couldn't breathe so I would sniffle.

For the entire first week I went only part of the day. Each day, my mom let me stay a little bit longer. Just like on that first day, my mom took me and Bailey to school and Mark Coleman picked me up. When I got home, my dad and I watched TV together while I colored in my coloring book.

After that first week, I stayed at school all day. Life began to settle into a routine. Things that once felt different started to become the new normal. I wore a hat every day for a long time, especially because the part of my head that had been shaved was growing new, pokey hairs.

Eventually, I was able to play basketball again. I ignored the doctor's request and did not wear a face mask because of my extreme fear of being made fun of even more. Although every time I got hit or ended up on the floor during a game, my mom jumped up out of the bleachers.

Every couple of days, I went to the hospital to visit my brother. A few weeks after the crash, he was sent to a rehab hospital where he would learn to walk again. He had nine surgeries total and multiple blood transfusions. One of the local churches held a blood drive for our family; I wasn't allowed to give blood.

Finally, my brother came home after three months of sleeping in hospital beds. He still had to go to outpatient physical therapy every day. He wasn't able to drive or do a lot of things on his own, so my mom had to help him. I don't think he wanted to drive though. He seemed afraid to even think about getting behind the wheel, and I definitely think he never wanted me to ride with him in a car again.

I was so glad when my brother came home, but he was a lot quieter than he had been before the crash. He didn't say much to me or pick on me as much. I'm sure he was in pain, but it looked like it was more than just his legs that hurt. Looking at him was like looking at eyes that held a secret behind them. It was as if he didn't see me when he looked at me, but he saw something or someone else. He stayed in his room a lot and he got tired easily.

He did come to some of my basketball games though. I loved seeing him out in the crowd. He usually sat on the front row because he wasn't able to climb up the bleachers. My brother wasn't one of those loud cheerleaders, but he always acted so proud of me. I felt a bit guilty because he wasn't able to run and play like I did. Even though he was happy for me, I couldn't help but wonder if he was upset about all of the things he wasn't able to do.

Mean Words

Things people say to me always stick with me. I remember the nice words and thoughtful cards, but I also recall the snide comments, hurtful words, and nasty glares. I knew I looked different. There was no denying that I had something on my face that was out of the ordinary. I understood that people stared because they weren't used to seeing someone with injuries on their face like mine. I didn't get mad when people looked at me longer than to simply smile. It didn't make me angry when people asked questions of what happened to me. It was when people said mean words that hurt my heart.

These words made me feel a little less of a person, every single time.

There was a superlative contest at school, in which people are nominated as the best of something in the school or in the class. The students vote on the nominees for a winner. There was Most Likely to Succeed, Most Athletic, Most School Spirit, Most Talkative, and the list goes on and on, classifying individuals into certain categories. One of my very best friends nominated me for Cutest Girl. Deep down I knew it was probably a pity vote because she wanted my name on the list, but that nomination meant the world to me. It made me feel like there were people who looked past my face and my scars and saw me for who I really am.

There were three other girls nominated from other classes. The final vote was set for the following week. Some of my opponents made posters and handed out flyers asking our classmates for their vote. I was just glad to be nominated, but I never thought I would actually win. A week later, when the votes were all tallied, much to my surprise they announced my name as the winner of "Cutest Girl." I couldn't stop smiling. I was so honored.

Later that day, after the announcement, I was standing at my locker and one of my friends came running toward me, "Kelly, Kelly, you'll never guess what this one girl said!"

"What did she say?"

My friend quickly told me, "She said, 'How did Kelly win Cutest Girl with a messed up face?'"

My heart sank to the pit of my stomach. I looked down at my feet, and I could feel my eyes starting to fill with tears. I took my backpack and sprinted to my aunt's office; the Art teacher at my middle school. By the time I got to her office, I had started blubbering, but I couldn't tell her what was wrong. She couldn't understand anything I said. My friend had followed me to my aunt's office and told her what that girl had said about me. My aunt wrapped her arms around me and held me until I was able to catch my breath.

My aunt let me sit in her office for a while, even when she had to go teach her class. Before I went back to class, my aunt told me that she was going to take care of the incident and for me not to think about it again. When I went back to class, everyone could tell that I had been crying. A lot of people asked me what was wrong. I said nothing.

I know people say mean words and aren't very nice, but I'll never understand why. Why did that girl have to say those mean things about me? Was it because her best friend didn't win?

There is the old saying about sticks and stones and words don't hurt; that's a lie. Words hurt. People try to say words don't hurt just to make themselves feel better. The truth is, what people say stays with you a lot longer than a broken bone or a bruise. I wish that girl could've said something nice; she didn't even know me. I wish that my friend would've stood up for me and would've told that girl that she shouldn't have said that. I also wish my friend wouldn't have told me the mean words that were said.

That girl will probably never know how much she hurt me. Years later, she probably doesn't even remember saying it. However, I remember. I know the influence her words had on my self-esteem. Those words always made me question myself.

The next day, I went to one of my teachers who was planning to give her a disciplinary action. I told the teacher not to worry about it. I knew that getting that girl in trouble because she hurt my feelings wouldn't make me hurt any less. I think some of the teachers did have a talk with her, but she never said she was sorry.

After this, I started making sure I said nice words to people. Who cares what someone is wearing or what they look like? Who cares that someone may be more quiet, or loud, or bigger, or smaller? Everyone is different which is what makes us who we are. No one is ugly. No one is stupid. Stupid and ugly really are mean words.

Swear to Tell the Truth

As time went on, I started pretending to be happy. I blamed myself for the wreck. I didn't like myself at all. I hated the way I looked, and I didn't know how to deal with all of the feelings inside me. I thought Satan had done this awful thing to me because my relationship with God was so strong; this made me afraid to pray. So, I didn't do anything except pretend to be okay, mentally, physically, and spiritually.

I soon recognized that making people laugh was one of my greatest gifts. I tried to make other people smile because it made me smile. Once other people started having fun around me, I felt like they liked me. However, I started losing myself and living behind a facade of who I thought people wanted me to be, instead of being who I really was. I didn't deal with any of my emotions; I just covered them up, layer after layer, year after year.

After a while, I became really good at not being honest with myself. I wasn't as close to God because I was afraid to be close to Him anymore. Part of me thought that something bad would happen to me or my family if I continued to grow in my relationship with Christ.

After about a year, my mom, brother, and I received subpoenas to appear in court to testify against the drunk driver, William Henson. I told my dad that I didn't believe in swearing so I wasn't going to tell them that I swore to tell the truth. He laughed and told me that in this situation it wasn't bad to swear. I told him that I wanted to promise instead of swear.

I dreaded the trial. I had never met the man I was testifying against, but I hated him. I hated what he did to me and my family. It made me angry that he took away a part of my life that I could never get back. I was dreading having to relive a past that I had tried so hard to forget.

The next two months I spent preparing for the trial. I gave multiple depositions and spoke with lawyers, going over questions that would be asked while I was on the stand. I was terrified. I didn't know why we had to go to court since we all knew he was guilty. Logically, this man should be found guilty, but what if, God forbid, that he is found innocent and was allowed out driving on the road again. I wasn't ready for that possibility.

There was a silver lining of hope in my heart that this drunk driver would go to court, plead guilty, and say he was sorry to my family, the judge, and the jury. I so badly wanted him to beg us for forgiveness because he knew that he had messed up. Maybe the few months he had already served in prison made him realize that he had made a horrible choice, the wrong choice. Maybe it was possible for him to want to change. Maybe he didn't want alcohol to be a part of his life anymore. I mean, it was possible.

Entering the courtroom was like walking into church late. Everyone turned their heads to see who was entering the door in the back of the courtroom. I felt like I had to tiptoe to my seat while trying to whisper and figure out where to sit.

Our whole family decided to sit together on the right side of the courtroom. I sat down but could hardly sit still. My leg kept bouncing up and down until my mom put her hand on it, signaling me to stop. We sat for a few minutes and then we heard a door in the front of the courtroom open. A police officer walked through it; a man followed after him. There he was, William McKinley Henson. I had never seen him before, but I knew it was him; the handcuffs were a dead giveaway. I couldn't help but stare at this man I didn't know. Despite everything I had been through, seeing him was the worst pain I ever felt in my life. There is no way to explain the amount of hurt I was going through just by seeing that man. I wondered what was going through his mind. Was he scared? Nervous? Depressed? I know I was depressed, mad, angry, upset, anxious, worried, and everything else. It was one of those times in my life when I wished I could curl up in a ball and become invisible.

As much as I didn't want to be there, I still couldn't stop looking at this man that I didn't even know. Mr. Henson just stared at the ground. I wanted him to look up at me. If he looked at me, maybe he could tell how much I was hurting. Maybe I could tell if he really was sorry, or if he felt any emotion. So many questions were going through my mind. Did he even know me? Did he know I was the little girl in the crash?

A voice broke my dazed stare, "All rise, the Honorable Judge Overstreet presiding. Court is now in session."

We stood as the judge, wearing a black robe, entered the courtroom and sat down in the big seat, front and center. "Please be seated and come to order."

The District Attorney assured me that this first day would be painless, for me at least, because I didn't have to do anything. On the first day, twelve lucky people in the courtroom would be chosen to serve their civic duty on the jury. They would be the ones deciding Henson's fate. Goodness, I hoped that they picked a group of twelve moral citizens who hated alcohol as much as I did. There seemed to be at least thirty juror candidates that the attorneys would weed through. I'm not sure any of them wanted to be there.

After four hours of questioning individuals about whether anyone was related to those involved with the case, whether they knew anything about the crash, and what moral and religious beliefs they held, the jury was selected. All who were not chosen left the courtroom. No one looked disappointed that they were not chosen to continue with the trial. The longer I sat there, the less nervous and scared I felt.

Boredom set in. Judge Overstreet banged his wooden gavel and gave us a break for lunch. The court recessed for an hour and would resume with opening statements.

When we returned from lunch, I wasn't allowed to go into the courtroom. I had to go to a different room. All of the witnesses for the prosecution were sent to a back room. The windowless room had a giant table in the center, lots of chairs, and a clock above the door. Eight of us were stuck in this small, cold, muggy room. We would sit there until our name was called. I felt like an old broomstick stuck in a closet that wouldn't be taken out until spring cleaning. It didn't appear that cleaning season was anywhere near.

The other witnesses waiting with me were Jimmy Baxter, deputies from the Sheriff's Department, the county detective, the brother of the woman who died in the crash, my mom, my brother, and the other girl who was in the car with us. The first day, we were in the room together for a few hours. None of our names were called.

I was confused about how I was supposed to feel. Everyone else was cutting up and making jokes, but I didn't feel like smiling. I thought everything about this case was very sad. I was relieved that this man was receiving the consequences for his actions, but it also was disheartening to think that we were pleading for him to spend the rest of his life in jail. I kept quiet and let everyone else talk.

The second day of the trial, I came prepared. My mom, brother, and I didn't even step into the courtroom. We walked straight into our little designated closet. My aunt helped to walk my dad into the courtroom to watch the trial. I brought my coloring books. I even brought extras in case I needed to share them. I had to have something to distract me, so I wouldn't start thinking too much and get nervous jitters. The other witnesses chuckled when they saw the activities I brought to occupy myself. However, after a few hours, most of them were envious that I had something to do instead of twiddling my thumbs. By lunchtime, none of us had been called to the witness stand. I started wondering what was going on with the case.

After the lunch recess, the prosecuting attorney called his first witness, Jimmy Baxter. He was the first guy on the scene, and he was in the truck that my brother had been following. I wish I could hear the questions that Mr. Baxter was being asked.

There were seven of us left in the cleaning closet. It didn't take long before they called the second witness for the prosecution, one of the deputies from the Sheriff's Department. Sadly, that was the last witness called for the second day of the trial. Court would adjourn until the next morning. When the bailiff came to tell us the news, my head dropped. I wasn't sure that I could handle another day of this.

The third day, my coloring book was tucked under my arm once again, even though my mom told me that I wouldn't need it. She promised me, and crossed her heart, that today was the day I would get called to the witness stand. I didn't know if I wanted today to be the day. Although I wanted it to be over with, I still wasn't ready. After a few witnesses for the prosecution had been called in the morning, there were four of us left in the waiting room; my brother, my mom, the county's detective, and myself. When the door opened, everyone's head jerked and stared, waiting for a name to be called.

"Kelly, they are ready for you." The bailiff held out his arm to lead me in the right direction. All I wanted to do was go back into the little waiting room, stand as still as possible, pretend to be a broom, and go unnoticed for the rest of the trial. I followed the bailiff from the back of the courtroom to the front where the judge was sitting. All eyes of the audience, the jury, and the judge were on me, except for William Henson's; and that's exactly where I kept looking. I wanted to see the man whom I had never met, but who had changed my life forever. I thought that finally seeing him would affirm my hatred toward him. Oddly enough, it didn't. Seeing his depressed glare up close made me realize that this man had no hope. He knew that his future would most likely be spent behind bars, with occasional visits allowed from his friends and family. I was conflicted because I knew he deserved it, but I also realized how depressing a life like that would be. I wonder what he thought when he saw me.

I tried to look out in the crowd to find my dad; he always made me feel better. Sitting alongside him were my grandparents, aunts, and friends who were also staring at me and putting on brave, smiling faces. Everything was going to be okay.

***

I walked up to the stand and sat down where the bailiff directed me. My legs wouldn't stop moving. I couldn't sit still. The bailiff came toward me and asked me to put my right hand in the air and my left hand on the Bible. Then he asked me to swear.

"Miss Kelly Samples, do you swear to tell the truth, the whole truth, and nothing but the truth, so help you God?"

Softly, I whispered, "I do."

Fielding Ballard, the prosecuting attorney, stood up from his seat, hiked up his britches, situated his tie, and walked toward me, "Miss Samples, will you please state your full name for the jury?"

"Kelly Elizabeth Samples."

"How old are you?"

"I'm fourteen."

"Are you nervous, Miss Samples?"

"I'm trying not to be, but a little."

Fielding Ballard paused for a moment, looked at the jury, then back at me. "Don't be nervous, Kelly. I am just going to ask you a few short, painless questions."

I didn't care what he asked me. I wanted to get this over with.

"Kelly, what were you doing on the night of July 23, 2004?"

"I was at my friend's house and we were having a bonfire."

"Who came to pick you up from the bonfire?"

"My brother, Matthew, and his girlfriend."

Mr. Ballard paused before his next question, "Kelly, do you remember anything about the wreck that you were in that night?"

"No sir."

"What is the last thing you remember after leaving the bonfire?"

"I remember trying to decide what song to listen to and then waking up in the hospital."

"What kind of injuries did the doctors say that you received from the crash?"

I took a deep breath because my voice was starting to shake. "The doctors said I had an enclosed head injury with a broken orbit around my eye, my sinus cavities were crushed on my left side, and I had a lot of facial lacerations along my forehead, cheek, and neck. There were a lot of cuts on my right shoulder, and many little injuries that I can't remember."

"Do you still have problems from your injuries that you suffered in the crash?"

"Yes, I still have a lot of issues with my sinuses. I had to get braces, because the wreck messed up my teeth. And, I still have to put medicine on my scars every day to try and make them go away. People stare at me all the time."

The prosecuting attorney could tell I was having a hard time. He looked at me and nodded his head, "That is all of the questions that I have for you, Miss Samples."

Next came the part that I was super freaked out about; it was the defense's turn to question me. I didn't have a clue what they would ask me. Judge Overstreet looked down from the bench and stated, "Defense, your witness."

Henson's lawyer had a mullet with a ponytail that I couldn't stop staring at. He stood up from sitting beside Mr. Henson and walked toward me. Mr. Henson finally looked up from the floor, and I looked him straight in the eyes. He immediately looked in the opposite direction, then back toward the ground, as if avoiding me completely.

Henson's lawyer said his name and introduced himself, but I really wasn't listening. Once I realized he was already asking me questions, I politely asked him to repeat what he asked.

"Kelly, can you tell me what grade you're in?"

"I'm in the ninth grade at Shelby County High School."

"What grade were you in when the wreck happened?"

"It was the summer before I started the eighth grade."

"I know you've already answered this, but I want to ask you again. Do you remember anything about the wreck?"

"No, I do not."

"So, you do not remember whether or not Mr. Henson was driving the other vehicle that was in the accident with you?"

I was stunned. That was such a mean, unfair question. Of course I don't remember who was driving the vehicle because I don't remember anything about the crash. But yes, Mr. Henson was driving. Who else could have been driving?

"No, I do not remember," I mumbled, fighting back tears.

"That is all of the questions the defense has for Miss Samples, Your Honor," Henson's lawyer proudly announced while turning his back to me and walking away.

Once the prosecution said there were no more questions for cross examination, the judge told me that I could exit the stand and have a seat next to my family. The bailiff gave me a tissue, then stuck out his hand to help me step down from the stand. I looked at the jury as I walked to my seat and couldn't help but wonder whether or not I had said anything wrong.

I sat down next to my dad. Everyone around patted me on the back and told me I had done a good job. Next, they called my mom to the stand. They asked her a bunch of questions about me and Matthew and everything we had to go through. She was on the stand a lot longer than I was.

After my mom completed her testimony, they called my brother to the stand. The prosecution asked him a lot of questions about the wreck since he remembered everything. It was weird though, because Henson's lawyer barely asked Matthew any questions about the wreck. Instead, they asked my brother lots of questions about our dad. Since my dad had been so involved with our county's emergency services, the defense was trying to make it seem like my brother and I may have gotten special treatment because we knew so many people that responded to the scene. However, that wasn't the case at all. My brother was confused about why they were asking him these questions.

The final witness that the prosecution called was Detective Jason Rice; he was the one who performed the reconstruction of the crash. Detective Rice gave a thorough explanation of the scene and what had been found. The end of his testimony was the worst part because they showed a video. It was a fifteen-minute film taken with the deputy's dash camera showing the aftermath of the wreck. The camera had been in Deputy Daniel Wills' vehicle, and he had a ride-along with him who took the camera out of the car at the scene.

The bailiff rolled a cart into the courtroom with a television and DVD player on it. He set it in front of the jury and turned out the lights.

The first eight minutes of the video was of the patrol car driving to the crash. You could hear the dispatcher's call come across the scanner, "Bagdad Road. There is a wreck with five people involved, three seriously injured, and two possible 1080's--dead people." The deputy's car engine revved up on each straight away and slowed down around each curve. It seemed to take forever for the officers to actually get to the scene. Eventually, the car stopped and parked off of the road behind another vehicle. Officers run toward the cars while people scream for medical bags.

Once the camera is taken out of the officer's car and moved toward the scene, you hear the sound of a child shrieking in terror for her life. That shrieking child was me. It sounded like it was out of a horror movie. It didn't sound like a real person. The sad thing was that the people on the scene said they were glad to hear that scream. It was when I stopped screaming and I wasn't making any sound that they were afraid I wouldn't make it.

You see two men holding my head as it was stuck through the windshield. Then you hear my brother scream out, "I'm so sorry!" He had absolutely nothing to be sorry for. There were more than a dozen people running around, trying to help. Briefly, you see Mr. Henson lying on the ground beside his car, next to the driver's door. There were boxes, a cooler, and cans of beer surrounding Henson's vehicle.

Next, the video switched to four hours after the crash, 4:00 a.m. All who were injured and the one deceased had been removed from the scene, but the vehicles remained. The cars were splattered with blood, covered with shattered glass, and completely smashed, never to be driven again. The scene looked like a bomb exploded and there were no survivors.

At the end of the video, the person filming walked backwards, away from the cars, so you could see the complete wreckage. It was like showing the final battle to the end of a war. However, my battles were just beginning.

When the television turned to a black screen, silence fell across the courtroom, except for the sniffles of those wiping away their tears. The lights turned on and there was nothing anyone could say.

"The prosecution rests, Your Honor," Fielding Ballard's voice quivered.

All of the witnesses had been seen. The attorneys were ready to give their closing arguments. The prosecution had a lot of diagrams drawn out on a jumbo legal pad that had been put up on an easel to show the jury the points that had already been stated. Henson's attorney summed up his points as well, but it seems like the defense's argument changed three separate times over the course of three days. At this point, all I could think about was what those twelve jurors were thinking. Once the closing arguments were completed, the judge instructed the jurors to file out the back of the courtroom where they would be escorted to a separate room. I tried to look at all of the jurors as they passed, trying to get one last look of sympathy.

They were walking away to decide this man's fate. His future was in their hands. Those twelve people would be the ones to decide the verdict of guilty or not guilty for William Henson.

The Verdict

One hour later, the twelve jurors filed back into the courtroom with the verdict. It seemed too quick for a decision. As the jurors walked in, those in the audience began to sit up a little straighter, straining their ears to listen a little better, and scooting toward the edge of their seats. This trial was coming to an end.

Then the lead juror read, "The jury finds the defendant, William McKinley Henson, guilty. William McKinley Henson is found guilty of one count of second degree manslaughter, three counts of second degree assault, driving under the influence of alcohol, driving without a license, and driving without proof of insurance."

A rush of relief came over me. I finally felt like it was over and I could breathe again. We wanted him to be found guilty. My family wanted him behind bars and pay the consequences for what he had done. I thought about what my brother and I had been through, and about the woman who died. Regardless of the time William Henson spent in jail, it wouldn't make up for what he had done. No matter how long he was behind bars, it wouldn't bring the dead woman back. She had two kids. Time wouldn't ever bring their mom back. I knew that he deserved his punishment. This wasn't his first offense.

I kept trying to remind myself of these awful things to make sure that I didn't feel any sympathy towards this man. I couldn't think about his family or his life. He didn't think about my life when he got behind the wheel drunk. I was having a constant battle within myself about how I was supposed to feel.

I started to leave the courtroom because I thought everything was over. My family quickly motioned for me to sit back down. It was time for the sentencing portion of the case. The jury would decide how long he would serve in prison for his guilty verdicts. Once again, the jury filed out through the back of the courtroom to their own room.

William Henson was escorted into a holding room so he wouldn't have to sit in the courtroom while waiting for his sentencing. After two hours, people started talking about calling to have pizza delivered. Nearly three hours had passed when we heard the back door of the courtroom open. The bailiff walked in, escorting the jury back to their seats. Once again, everyone in the courtroom fell silent.

The lead juror stood up for the last time and read, "William McKinley Henson is sentenced to twenty years for second degree manslaughter, twenty years for each count of second degree assault, and four months for being a repeated felon."

Holy cow! He was sentenced to prison for a total of more than eighty years.

The jury was escorted out of the courtroom for the final time. The judge banged his gavel, and court was adjourned. It was over. William Henson walked out in handcuffs and was taken back to his cell, which is where he would remain for a really long time. He never said he was sorry, and he never testified for himself.

Attorney Fielding Ballard came over to explain to our family that William Henson would not be serving all eighty years of his sentence. Since he received all second degrees in his verdict, he could not serve the full penalty. The most time he would serve in prison would be fifteen years. My mom started getting upset. My brother put his arm around her to try to calm her down. Together, our family stood up, walked out of the courtroom, and headed for home. Even though I wouldn't have to spend any time in bars like William Henson, I felt like a prisoner. I was mad, angry, and sad. He took away a part of my life, something that I would never get back. It wasn't fair. As a little girl, my mom always told me, "Life isn't fair; deal with it." I never believed her until this moment. I felt trapped behind invisible bars, like everything was holding me back even though there seemed to be nothing in front of me.

Time Doesn't Heal All Pain

It had been over three years since the wreck. People told me that things would get better with time, but that isn't true. Time doesn't heal pain or make hard times go away. Time is what it takes to get used to living with pain. Over time, I had grown to be more resilient or maybe it was just me trying to ignore every part of my past. I still hadn't gone to counseling nor talked to anyone about how I felt. Three years was long enough for the wreck to be something that people didn't talk about anymore. It was part of the past. However, for me, it was very much still in the present. It has defined who I am.

Scars were still on my face, and I continued to have nightmares. Right before school started, I got a haircut with dramatic bangs to help cover up my scars. There was the occasional person who asked what happened to my face. Each time, it still dug at me a little deeper. I begged my mom to take me to see a plastic surgeon. She finally agreed.

We scheduled a consultation. As soon as I walked into the plastic surgeon's office, I felt self-conscious, like people were judging the reason that I was there. I just wanted to schedule a surgery to make my scars go away. When my name was called, I went back and waited for the doctor. As he came in for his assessment, he pressed against the scars on my forehead and brushed the ones on my cheek. He didn't take very long with me.

The words of the doctor stung. "There is no kind of surgery I can perform that will help. The only thing that I could do is shave down this bump in the middle of your forehead, but I am afraid the incision will make it appear even worse. Plus, you're still at such a young age that I have no idea what kind of growth you have left. Continued growth will change the appearance of your scars completely. I am sorry, but there is nothing I can do."

My heart was crushed once again. I thought maybe the plastic surgeon would help erase a part of my past that I so badly wanted to forget. I couldn't even look the doctor in the eyes. My head sank as I walked out of the doctor's office with my eyes filled with tears. I felt hopeless. I still didn't understand why this happened to me. My mom told me that we could get a second opinion, but I didn't want that. I was mentally and emotionally exhausted.

The next morning I woke up, looked in the mirror, brushed back my hair, and stared at my scars. It was time for me to realize that these scars were not a curse. They were a gift from God. I had to learn to be proud of my scars because of the story they told. They're my battle scars.

Still looking at myself in the mirror, I decided that every time I saw my scars they would serve as a reminder that God has a purpose for my life. He wasn't ready for me to die. I had survived a traumatic event. After that, every day got a little easier. I had to start loving who I was. I was proof that God still performs miracles, and I should at least love myself for that. Time was passing, I was getting older, and I had to learn to deal with the pain.

It's Not Worth It

Turning sixteen is a huge milestone in any teenager's life. This is the moment when your whole life is supposed to change. You are given responsibilities, gain more freedom, and get your driver's license! When my sixteenth birthday finally came, it wasn't as exciting as I imagined it would be. I was excited to be able to drive, but I was also terrified of having a crash like the one when I was twelve. Even though I was doing all of the right things behind the wheel, it doesn't mean that the person in the other car was.

After I got my license, things started changing. I started going to more places and staying out later on Friday and Saturday nights. I noticed that I wasn't the only one changing. My friends were different, as well. Priorities changed. Most conversations were about where the party would be held on the weekend and who would bring the beer.

I was naïve and pretty sheltered. I didn't know people my age started drinking alcohol in high school. I didn't think kids under twenty-one got drunk. To me, drinking was illegal. I knew I wasn't supposed to do it. But it seemed like everyone else was doing it.

On weekends, I would go out with my friends and people would pull alcohol from the closets or go to their cars to get it. I was super uncomfortable, because I didn't know how I felt about it. In my household, alcohol was always taboo. If you mentioned it, it was like talking about the devil.

Every single time I saw my best friends drinking alcohol, I sat back and watched it happen. I watched drunken friends jump over fires, tipsy girls get taken advantage of, and people fall over when trying to walk straight. As I sat and watched so many people acting like idiots, there were other people who thought it was hilarious. The thing I hated the most about watching their behavior was that I did absolutely nothing.

Every single time I was around my friends while they drank alcohol, I was scared. All I could think about was the man sitting behind bars and the pain me and my family suffered. I knew none of my friends would purposely hurt themselves or anyone else. My friends weren't bad people. My friends were good people, but what if something happened? What if they thought they were okay to drive, but weren't, and ended up hurting a twelve year-old girl, or killing someone, or killing themselves?

One time, I remember one of my very best friends getting so drunk and ended up passing out in the shower with the water running, lying in vomit. I kept trying to call, but this friend didn't answer. Times like these were when I was terrified that my friends would die from alcohol poisoning. I didn't want to make them mad by telling them I was worried or that I thought their drinking was wrong. I didn't want to look like a loser, but I also didn't want anyone to have to go through what I had gone through.

I realized that William Henson didn't get behind the wheel that night and purposefully crash. He didn't mean to kill his girlfriend and he didn't mean to hurt me or my brother. William Henson made a bad choice; one bad choice that would never go away.

As a junior in high school, getting ready to go to prom, I decided to tell my story. The school Resource Officer, Gena Johnson, asked my brother if he would like to speak the day before prom in front of the junior and senior class and talk about the wreck. When my brother graciously turned down the opportunity, I decided that I was tired of not saying anything. It was my turn to speak.

I planned on going to my junior prom with my high school sweetheart, Ben McNew. I wanted to make sure everyone there would make the right choices. All of the juniors and seniors who were going to prom were called to the gym for an assembly. I had written down what I planned to say on index cards. As my name was called to walk to the microphone, I could barely stand up straight. My legs were shaking and my arms were fidgety. As I turned around behind the podium, all I could see were 500 pairs of eyes staring back at me, waiting for me to say something insightful. I tried to read from my cards but I couldn't stop stuttering. I went through a few index cards until my words started to come out smoothly. Once the words came, the tears flowed right along with them.

This was really the first time I had ever told the story of being hit by a drunk driver. I poured out my heart, begging my classmates to never drink and drive because it's not worth it. It's not worth a parent losing a child, or a child losing a parent. It's not worth losing your best friend. It's not worth the risk. Life isn't worth losing over one bad choice.

As I finished my story and returned to my seat in the audience, I wondered how many people actually listened. I prayed that everyone heard me. I hoped that my classmates would make the right decisions on prom night and every night after that.

Telling
My
Story

A few years after telling my story to the junior and senior class at my high school, I decided that I wanted to tell my story to everybody. I wanted to use what happened to me to help other people. So I started calling local high schools, asking if I could come and speak to students before their prom. I also was invited to speak at the Kentucky State Reformatory, to a men's substance abuse class.

Every place that I went to speak was different. At the high schools, a lot of students would tell me their own stories of being hit by a drunk driver. Some kids would tell me how they were worried about their mom, dad, brother, sister, or other relative who they knew got behind the wheel drunk. Occasionally, kids would come up and tell me how they had driven drunk before and that they would never do it again. I never knew what to expect, especially when speaking at the prison.

When I walked into the Kentucky State Reformatory, I was scared. I was speaking in front of criminals who may have been convicted of the same crime that William Henson was. I was speaking from the victim's perspective, and I was sure that was something they didn't hear very often. The group of twenty men surprised me. They clung to every word of my story. Then they shared their stories with me. Almost all of them admitted to getting behind the wheel drunk. Their explanations were that they just weren't thinking. It's what they had always done. They never thought about the other people on the road and the consequences of their actions.

One guy in the crowd asked me if I had ever talked to the drunk driver, William Henson. All I could say was, "No." I had never spoken to him and had never seen him since the trial. He had gone up for parole once but was denied. He was up for parole again soon. Those guys in prison challenged me to think about writing William Henson a letter or trying to talk to him. These men explained that they sit behind bars every single day, thinking about the crimes they committed. They told me it may help the drunk driver to hear from me. He may even want to contact me, but was scared to.

Before going to the prison to speak, I had never thought about trying to contact the drunk driver. I never imagined that he would want to hear from me. For years, I had wondered what he was thinking or if he was sorry, but I never thought about just asking him. It did scare me to think about him getting out on parole. I didn't know what I would do if he got out and I ran into him in our small town. I wouldn't know what to say. I felt there was so much more that I should say even before he got out of prison. It wasn't easy thinking about him possibly being out on the road again, but that was very possible. It felt like it was my responsibility to say something, for me, for my brother, and for my family. So, I decided to write William Henson, the drunk driver, a letter.

Dear Mr. Henson,

It's been over eight years and I've never gotten the chance to properly introduce myself. My name is Kelly Samples, and I've wanted to talk to you for a really long time. I'm the little girl who was in the crash on July 23, 2004.

I have no clue what I should say. Sometimes I sit and wonder if you ever think about that night and what happened. I always question whether or not you are remorseful. However, for a long time I have wanted to tell you that I've forgiven you. Some things I will never fully understand. I still do not know why anyone would drink and drive, but I hope you've been able to learn from what happened. I have no feelings of hatred toward you and I am no longer bitter.

I would really like to hear from you because, other than your name, I have no clue who you really are. So please, feel free to write back. For these eight years, I've had to deal with wondering what you are thinking.

It has taken me a while to gain the courage to write this letter. Now I hope you realize how much you've affected my life. I've forgiven but never will forget. My final statement is that I beg for you to never drink and drive again for as long as you live.

Sincerely,
Kelly Samples

Henson's Reply

After letting my brother read the letter, I stuffed it into an envelope, put a stamp on it, but held on to it. I packed that letter around for a couple of days before I finally dropped it in the mailbox. For me this was my final goodbye. I was letting go of the wreck. I was using this letter as a way to find my closure. After sending the letter, I put everything about the wreck as far out of my mind as possible.

One week after sending the letter, my phone rang. I didn't recognize the Bagdad number but I answered anyway.

"Hello."

"Hi Kelly, this is Angie. William called me and said that he got your letter."

I was confused. *Who is Angie? Wait, who is William? What letter was she talking about?* Then it hit me. I realized that William had read my letter. It had only been one week to the day since I sent the letter to the drunk driver. I never thought he would respond or that I would hear from him, especially this quickly. I had said my peace and I was ready to move on. Evidently, he felt like he was ready to say his peace as well. Angie was calling to relay a message.

Angie was from Bagdad, and she worked at the local store. She told me that she and William Henson had been together for nearly ten years before the wreck. They had broken up about a year before it happened. Once he was in prison, the two started writing back and forth. She tries to visit him almost every Sunday. They were trying to work things out. Until this phone call, I had no clue they had any sort of connection.

Angie continued talking about everything William had told her. He had read her the letter and was excited to hear from me after all of these years. She kept going on and on about how he thinks about the wreck every day, how he is a changed person, and how this had been an eye-opening experience for him. She told me that he was really working hard in prison and things were going to be different when he got out.

Then she said, "Kelly, he wanted to write you back, but he doesn't know how to write very well. He doesn't feel like he can get all that he wants to say in a letter. He wants to talk to you. The only two ways we can arrange this is for you to come over to my house and he can call you on my house phone, because he can only call certain numbers. Or we can try and arrange a special visit."

"What kind of special visit do you mean?"

"Well, we could arrange for you to go to the prison, Blackburn Correctional Complex, to sit down and talk with him, face to face. I could go with you if you want. I am not sure which option you feel more comfortable with, but it is something for you to think about."

Without hesitation, I knew what I wanted to do. "I want to go talk with him in person. I don't mind if you're there, too."

This didn't seem real. I was going to meet the man who changed my life. This was something I had to do. I was terrified to do it, but I knew that I had to meet him. It just wouldn't be the same to have a phone conversation. I wanted to look him in the eyes, and I wanted him to have to look into mine.

Angie continued by telling me what would happen next, "I'm going to visit him on Sunday, so I can talk with him more about it then. After that, I will give you a call and tell you what we have to do to plan a visit. So, I'll talk to you sometime next week."

We said our thank you and goodbyes, and that was it. I couldn't believe what had just happened. Never in my wildest dreams would I have thought that William Henson would want to talk with me and meet me. I was skeptical, anxious, excited, nervous, and not the least bit ready for meeting a man that I had only thought of as a drunk. Part of me was afraid he would change his mind and back out. Part of me wanted him to back out. I didn't know how to feel, act, or think. All I knew was that there was no way that I was going to tell my mom that I planned on going to prison to meet the drunk driver.

It's Actually Happening

Eight days later, my phone rang with the same unknown Bagdad number showing up on the screen. I went to press the answer button and it stopped ringing. I had just missed the call from Angie. I immediately pressed the call back button. The phone started ringing, ringing, and ringing.

Finally, she answered, "Hello."

I quickly responded, "Hi, Angie."

"Oh, hey Kelly, I'm so glad you called me back. Did you get any paperwork in the mail last week from the prison?"

"No, I have no clue what you're talking about."

"William said that you are scheduled to visit with him tomorrow. Can you make it then?"

"Tomorrow??"

There was a long pause. Angie could have been saying something, and I would not have heard it. I couldn't believe I was supposed to meet him the very next day. I didn't feel prepared. Seeing William Henson was supposed to be like finding the end of the rainbow. You always say that you'll do it but it never really happens.

I stuttered, "Um … I may be able to make it tomorrow. Are you going to be home the rest of the night?"

"Yeah, I'll be at home."

I told her I would give her a call back in a little while.

As soon as I hung up the phone, I called Ben, my boyfriend of five years. I wanted him to tell me what to do. He didn't answer my call the first time, so I called him again. He answered and sounded hurried, "Kelly, what's going on?"

"Angie called me."

"Who?" He had no clue what I was talking about.

"The lady who knows William Henson and goes to visit him. She said I'm scheduled to visit him at the prison tomorrow. What should I do?"

He calmly answered, "I guess you should go visit him at the prison tomorrow."

"Ben, I don't know if I can do this. Will you take me?"

"Yes, I will take you." He had to go, so we hung up. This was actually happening.

I waited a few hours to call Angie back. By the end of the evening, I called and told her that I would be there the next day. I was supposed to be at the prison that next morning, nine o'clock on September 9, 2012. I had fifteen hours until I would meet the man who changed my life forever.

That Sunday

I was up before the sun. My parents had barely
gotten out of bed when I left the house. I didn't
want to have to tell them where I was going. I didn't
want them to know. I just said I was going
somewhere with Ben. My brother knew that I had
been thinking about going to the prison, but he
didn't know I was going that Sunday. I had asked
him if he wanted to go, even though I knew he
would say no.

I met Ben, hopped into his car, and we
headed to the prison an hour away. I had looked up
the directions so I thought I knew where we were
going. We found the prison and I was a bit

intimidated by the high walls and razor wire. Ben waited in the car while I stood in the long line to get inside. Thirty minutes later, I was told that I was at the wrong prison. I was mortified. I couldn't believe that I went to the wrong place.

Ben was surprised to see me get back into the car so quickly. He didn't believe me when I told him we were at the wrong place. The prison we were supposed to go to was another half mile down the road. One of the guards gave me directions, so we headed that way.

Once we were at the right prison, our car was searched and we showed our IDs to the guard. Ben wasn't allowed to stay on the premises since he wasn't going inside, so he dropped me off and said, "Good luck." He knew I was nervous. I was also scared. I had never been to a prison before to visit someone.

I walked slowly, very slowly, to the visitation building. I continued on the long winding sidewalk. Looking back, I could no longer see Ben's car. The prison didn't look at all like I had imagined it. There were no metal detectors to walk through, and there was no officer walking me around. When I came to the door, I paused, took a deep breath, and barely cracked it open. I peeked through the small opening and saw many people sitting inside. It was so loud. There were small tables set up around the room. Almost every table was full. There was a check-in table with three officers behind it. I signed a visitor's form and handed it to one of the officers. I awkwardly stood, not knowing what to do. The officer stared at me and finally said, "You can sit down at a table and wait." They had to get William Henson and bring him to the visitation area.

I turned to take a seat but didn't know where to go. I didn't know which table to pick, so I went to the bathroom. In the bathroom, I bowed my head to say a little prayer that God would help me through this. I wanted Him to calm my nerves, to let me be without fear, and to give me the right words to say. I wanted Him to not let me seem angry but to be able to show my forgiveness. I prayed for God to be right there with me.

When I walked out of the bathroom, I sat down at table twenty-four, my favorite number. I waited, staring at the hallway that William Henson would walk down. My head was filled with thoughts and questions that I wanted to ask, with things I needed to say. Then I felt a tap on my shoulder. I turned and saw a guard behind me. He said, "You can't sit anywhere you want. You have to sit at the table that you are assigned to."

I told the guard that I had no clue and no one had told me where to sit. The guard led me to table eighteen, and I sat down in the seat he pointed to. He told me that I was supposed to sit on the right side and the prisoners sit on the left side. I thought there would be glass between me and Henson. I didn't know we would be an arm's reach away from each other. There I sat, just waiting, thinking, and waiting.

As I waited, Angie walked in and checked in at the security desk. She was supposed to come visit him after me, but since I was late I messed up our plan. In just a few moments, she had pulled up a chair next to me to sit at table eighteen.

Once Angie sat down, she started talking about Henson. She told me what he had been doing while in prison, how often they got to talk and see each other, and their shared past. The more she talked about him, I started to realize that she was in love with this man. She cared for him in a way that I hadn't imagined possible. It was hard for me to think of him not as just a criminal, but as a person who has people on the outside of those cell walls who love him and care for him.

When I looked up; there he was.

Then he saw me. He looked toward the closest guards and pointed toward the wall. Then he disappeared, and I wondered what was going on. Twenty seconds later, he came back into the hallway where Angie and I could see him again. Next, I saw Henson lean toward a guard and whisper something to him. The guard started walking toward our table with William Henson following behind him. This was going nothing like I expected.

The guard asked me to stand up and walk to a different table, one that was in the very back corner of the room. This was my third table of the day. Supposedly, he had told the guard that he wanted us to be able to talk in privacy with no one else around. We walked to the table, and William Henson and I were alone. Angie had gone to the bathroom and the guard left us.

I held out my hand to introduce myself. He stuck his hand out to shake mine, but I couldn't even get out my name. Henson immediately said, "I'm so sorry. I wish I could take it all back. I'm just so sorry." Finally, I received the apology I had waited so long to hear.

We sat down together at this tiny table, a foot away from one another, and started talking. I think both of us were in shock at first and weren't sure what to say. I was meeting the man who had made a huge impact on my life for the past eight years. The man I had once hated but had come to forgive. Before this moment, he was a complete stranger whom I knew nothing about. I had so many unanswered questions.

He answered every single question that I asked. He told me everything. The day of the wreck he had been in West Virginia for a job. He and the guys he worked with had just gotten back and were relaxing. They were drinking. Then he remembered that he wanted to be home in his own bed. Other than that, he said he couldn't remember anything about that night. He even asked me if I remembered anything.

He told me about of all the injuries he suffered from the crash. He asked me how I was doing. He told me the plans he had once he would get out of prison.

Then he said, "I have never understood why I wasn't the one to die that night. There were so many other nights when I was drunk on my motorcycle and I came so close to hitting someone. I always ended up okay. Why did something happen that night?"

The only response I knew was to tell him, "God has a purpose for everything."

He looked me in the eyes and told me, "Kelly, in your letter you wrote me, you asked me to never drink and drive again. Well, I'm going to do you one better. I am never going to drink alcohol again."

I didn't believe him. He knew I didn't believe him. All I did was stare at him because I didn't know what else to say. Henson explained, "I've been drinking alcohol since I was a teenager. All it has done is cause me trouble. Nothing good has come out of it, so I'm done."

I looked at him, "Someone is going to have to hold you accountable."

He didn't pause, "No one is going to have to hold me accountable. This is my own decision."

I tried changing the subject and asked him what he had been doing in prison. Henson said that he was trying to learn to read and write better. He was taking classes. He told me, "These classes that they have here in prison, and the programs that I've gone through, they are only temporary. But do you know the only thing that lasts? AA (Alcoholics Anonymous) is what you stick with forever."

Henson was right. Alcoholism is something that would follow him around like a shadow for the rest of his life. He would have to deal with it every single day. It might be possible for him to never drink alcohol again. I just wish I would've told him that he didn't have to do it alone. God would stick with him and He was the only one who could truly help. My only regret is not using that moment to tell Henson about God.

I think Henson was optimistic about getting out. He wanted to make sure that I knew, "When I get out of here, if you or your brother ever need help with anything, you can always call me. If you all ever need help, I will try to do it for you. No matter what time of the day or night it is. I feel like I owe you and Matthew my life. There isn't a day that goes by that I don't think about you all. I just wish it wouldn't have ever happened."

We talked about so much. I really got to know him, past his name and past the fact of being a felon. About thirty minutes passed as we talked. One of the guards came over to our table and tapped me on the shoulder, "Ma'am, your ride is here."

Ben was waiting outside for me, so I stood up from my chair. I waited by the table while Henson continued to talk. I don't think he expected me to leave so soon. Before I left, he told me that he was very thankful that I had come and that he had the chance to meet me.

Then he looked me in the eyes and said, "I promise you that that I will never drink alcohol again."

All I could do was trust him and hope that he was telling me the truth. There was no way that I could ever really know if he drank alcohol again. There was no pencil and paper around us so I could get his word in writing.

I did the only thing I knew to do, I looked him right back in the eyes and stuck out my pinky, "Do you Pinky Promise?"

He chuckled, grinned really big, and stuck out his pinky to lock with mine, "I Pinky Promise!"

Our pinky fingers shook and we made the ultimate promise. I turned to leave without saying another word.

The Pinky Promise

I walked out of the prison that day and made Pinky Promises to myself. I Pinky Promised that I would try to stop anyone from driving under the influence of drugs or alcohol. I Pinky Promised that I would try to make the right decisions and do the right things. I didn't want to mess with drugs or alcohol, and I didn't want them to be a part of my life.

We make choices every day. Some choices are simple, while others are more difficult. Regardless of how little or big the choice is, it is something that stays with you for the rest of your life. One drink, one time using a drug, or one time getting behind the wheel drunk could be the choice that destroys your life. It doesn't take a million wrong choices, or a bunch of bad decisions, it takes only one.

I hope you care enough about yourself to want to make the right decisions. There are so many people in this world who care about you and love you, even if you don't think there are. Some people say you can be anything you want to be or do anything you want to do. I believe that you can be anything and do anything that God wants you to do. If you try to live your life for God, then everything else will fall into place. Bad things may still happen. Life isn't easy. But it's a whole lot better when you know you're never alone. God is always with you and will always love you.

There is something we can learn from every experience. My dad can now tell people that God is real and Heaven is an actual place. I can tell people that God has a plan for my life; a purpose that goes far beyond who I was at twelve years old. I have seen bad stuff happen first hand. I know good things can come from bad stuff. People aren't bad, they just make bad choices.

Think about your life. Think about the choices you've made, you're going to make, and what you want your story to be.

What is your Pinky Promise?

The Christmas after Dad's heart attack,
December 2002.

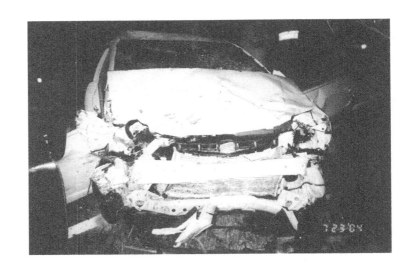

My brother's car in the crash.

The drunk driver's car in the crash.

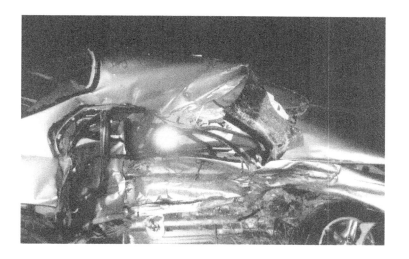

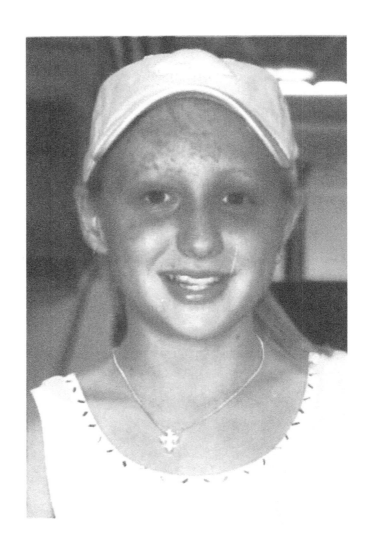

Two months after the crash,
September 2004.

Dad walking me down the aisle
on my wedding day,
September 6, 2014.

Me and my husband, Benjamin John McNew.

William Henson walked out of the prison on
May 2, 2016. I arranged to meet with him and his
parole officer one week later. As we sat around a
small room, I reminded him of the pinky promise he
had made four years earlier, and I spoke of the
thousands of others that had shared this pinky
promise since then. I wish him the best as he starts
to write this new chapter of his life. I know that I
am excited to see what God has planned for the next
chapter of mine.

14640119R10125